THE
NO
JOURNAL

Cynthia,
   I pray God continues
to bless you in your singleness!
May your yes mean yes &
your no mean no!

   Love, MEOCHIA

THE
NO
JOURNAL

90-DAYS OF SAYING NO TO MESS AND STRESS AND YES TO YOUR SUCCESS

MEOCHIA NOCHI
THOMPSON

Blessed Pen Ink

The No Journal

Copyright © 2022 Meochia Nochi Thompson

ISBN-10 978-0-9740777-5-8

Blessed Pen Ink Publishing is a division of Meochia Nochi Blount Publishing

Blessed Pen Ink Publishing
Join us at www.blessedpenink.com.
Write to inspire@blessedpenink.com.

Cover, Jacket Design, and Illustrations by Blessed Pen Ink Publishing

Printed in the United States of America

While the author has made every effort to provide accurate telephone numbers, Internet addresses, and other contact information at the time of publication, neither the publisher nor the author assumes any responsibility of errors, or for changes that occur after publication. Further, the publisher does not have any control over and does not assume any responsibility for author or third-party websites or their content.

Except for friends and family, names and identifying characteristics of individuals mentioned have been changed to protect their privacy.

This book is dedicated to my compassionate, Little, Beautiful Butterfly, Meochia Aponi; three special ladies, Ms. Vaughn, Momma Jean, and Ms. Harriett, who came into my life after the death of my mother; and all the people with giving hearts to encourage you to stand up for yourselves, not apologize for your pure hearts but learn to protect them.

Contents

INTRODUCTION

If you picked up this journal, you are probably tired of saying yes or feeling guilty when you say no to people and their seemingly nonstop requests. That was me. I was a push over or what I have termed, a "dumping ground". It was hard for me to say no to anybody about almost anything. Well, there were some things that I absolutely stood my ground on, besides those, my stomach would be in knots worried about what the other person thought or what terrible things would happen if I didn't give in. Or I sometimes wondered if God would be angry with me for saying "no". I found this "no" problem went beyond my family. That's how I knew it wasn't really a people issue, it was a me issue.

A pleaser or a giver can have a hard time saying no at home, church, school, in relationships or anywhere else. That is a part of who I am or who we are. It isn't a bad thing, but it could become a problem when people begin to take too much, or we start to feel like we are giving too much. Or we begin feeling used or negative towards the receiver. There could be many reasons we are wired the way we are. I like to think God just made us this way, but some things can stem from deeper issues like neglect, rejection, esteem, and abuse.

It is important to understand why you do what you do or why you are wired a certain way because that helps you find a base of how to assist you in your "NO" journey. I've found a good therapist can help and some exercise in utilizing your "no" power. For me, I did suffer some abuse as a child, which led to some feelings of rejection, as well as disconnection issues as an adult. It was easier for me to stand up for others rather than myself. I didn't want anyone else to feel sad, so I took a lot of abuse that I shouldn't have because I felt like I could take it or even sometimes like I deserved it. These issues made me work extra hard to get things right. I wanted to be the best but most importantly, I didn't want to disappoint anyone. I kept in contact with people who took me for granted like I deserved their bogus behavior, and I couldn't understand why I attracted them or couldn't easily pull away from them. I was so accustomed to this type of negativity that I was comfortable with it.

This "pleasing" type of behavior spilled over into my marriage. I had to learn how to speak up for what I wanted instead of always submitting to everyone in the house. I couldn't even pick my own movie at the theatre. I would watch what they wanted to see. In my heart I wanted to look at something different, but I wouldn't say it when asked. I thought I had a superiority complex, but it wasn't that simple. It was more like my needs were inferior to everyone else because again, "I could take it."

There are other places that could catch a "pleaser" off guard. In ministry, we become "yes people". We say yes to everything leadership asks us to do. We think we are doing it to please God until it starts becoming a burden and regret sets in. At this point, feelings of guilt start to arise. Usually, we pull away from ministry and sometimes the church all together because we are too afraid to say no. Well, I learned how to pray over everything I was asked to do before I committed.

Now, when someone says, "Do you think you can help with...?"

My first response is, "Let me pray about it and get back to you."

God is not on your time clock, so if it takes a while, it just does. If there is a deadline and you still don't feel God has given you an answer, you might have to just say no until he shows you otherwise.

At school and work, performance is important. These are places where you form friendships and lasting relationships. It's easy to get caught up in multiple projects and activities that soak up a lot of time and if you aren't careful, it could easily spill over into your personal life. We must protect our personal time and space. Here, I had to learn how to tell my supervisors if I was too busy or be realistic about project completion. If I was working on an assignment with a team, I had to learn not to take on the work of people who slacked. I wanted a good grade. Again, I felt if they didn't do the work, I had to. Taking on extra work doesn't help the other person learn and it adds extra stress to you. I had to learn how to take a deep breath, tell the other person I was not going to do their work for them, and go to the teacher if me and my teammate couldn't get on the same page. Standing up for ourselves can be scary, it takes lots of courage but it's worth it.

Saying yes is easy but saying no becomes easier, especially if you want to protect yourself and be more available to say yes to other things.

This journal is your opportunity to learn how to say no. It's nice and simple. It's filled with wisdom and affirmations to get you started on your journey to more yeses in the future. That's right, the more you learn how to say no and stick by it, the more you will be open to say yes to what you really want to and need to do. For instance, if you're a parent, if you say no to picking up your kids coats every time they leave them laying on the balcony or wherever they throw them when they come home, and make them hang them in the closet, you can say yes to a few extra minutes of talking about their day before they run to their rooms to do homework. They learn to hang their own coats and you get to find out what is going on in their lives! It takes some getting used to and it may seem small, but all that discipline adds up to some healthy habits for everyone.

HOW IT WORKS

In this journal, you will have 90-Days to say "no" at least once a day and write down why you said it, how it made you feel, and tell what you were able to say yes to as a result. Each day comes with a bit of wisdom or an affirmation, a simple prayer to speak your heart, and a scripture that coincides.

You can do this! Say yes to finding your no and say yes to finding yourself because this world has been lost without the true you! By the way, you are something special. You will finish. You are amazing for all you do for others, and you are worthy of every gift God offers for your goodness! You don't deserve to be anyone's dumping ground. You deserve appreciation and some tender loving, self-care. When you finish this journal, read through it, and reflect on it. If you find yourself slipping into old habits, you can always start all over again. It's easy to say yes to everyone else, now it's time for you to say yes to you by starting your 90-Days to saying no journal! See you at the finish line!

The Start

DAY 1

To a pleaser saying the word "No" is like exercising a weak muscle, it hurts at first and you want to quit but after a while the results start showing. They look so good you wonder why you didn't do it sooner. Know why it is important for you to say no and trust your reasons even if nobody else understands.

Today, I said no to:

_____

_____

_____

_____

_____

Why did I say no?

_____

_____

_____

_____

_____

Saying no made me feel:

- o Independent
- o Strong
- o Guilty
- o Mean
- o Happy
- o Empowered
- o _____

My no gave me more:

- ○ Time
- ○ Opportunity
- ○ Satisfaction
- ○ Power
- ○ Anxiety

I am now available to say yes to or to do:

_____

_____

_____

_____

_____

Prayer

Lord, give me the strength to exercise my right to say no. I need to heal from my need to please and not disappoint. Lord, You help me to look to You for strength in my areas of weakness so I can be healthy and strong like those in my life need me to be. In Jesus' name. Amen.

Exodus 15:26 (NKJV)

And said, "If you diligently heed the voice of the LORD your God and do what is right in His sight, give ear to His commandments and keep all His statutes, I will put none of the diseases on you which I have brought on the Egyptians. For I am the LORD who heals you."

DAY 2

Remove the guilt of saying no to something you know is for someone's own good. You have your reasons, trust them. If the person has an issue with your no, give them space to reflect on how many times you said yes.

Today, I said no to:

_____

_____

_____

_____

_____

Why did I say no?

_____

_____

_____

_____

_____

Saying no made me feel:

- o   Independent
- o   Strong
- o   Guilty
- o   Mean
- o   Happy
- o   Empowered
- o   _____

My no gave me more:

- ○ Time
- ○ Opportunity
- ○ Satisfaction
- ○ Power
- ○ Anxiety

I am now available to say yes to or to do:

_____

_____

_____

_____

_____

Prayer

I cannot do everything on my own, Lord, I need You. Please prick my heart when I start making things about me and taking on things that I should not. I cannot do Your job, but I trust that You will do a job well done, even when I don't understand. Lord, You went through so much pain for my salvation, I know I can get through this. In Jesus' name, I thank You. Amen.

Isaiah 53:5 (KJV)

But he was wounded for our transgressions, he was bruised for our iniquities; the chastisement for our peace was upon him, and by his stripes we are healed.

DAY 3

Don't mind those who are angry at your no. They are like a baby throwing a temper tantrum. Of course, you wouldn't let a child touch a hot stove just because they wanted to. You know the pain and damage it will cause. Treat everyone the same way, if you know there is danger ahead the best thing you can do is block them from it with a big, fat, whopping, NO! Now, you say it.

Today, I said no to:

_____

_____

_____

_____

_____

Why did I say no?

_____

_____

_____

_____

_____

Saying no made me feel:

- ○ Independent
- ○ Strong
- ○ Guilty
- ○ Mean
- ○ Happy
- ○ Empowered
- ○ _____

My no gave me more:

- ○ Time
- ○ Opportunity
- ○ Satisfaction
- ○ Power
- ○ Anxiety

I am now available to say yes to or to do:

_____

_____

_____

_____

_____

PRAYER

Lord, I feel so much pain when I am labeled as the "bad guy", but I thank You for seeing the good in me. I will take those hits because You will heal and restore me and one day, they will see that Your wisdom has directed me to keep them from falling. Thank You, in Jesus' name. Amen.

Jeremiah 30:17 (NKJV)

'For I will restore health to you and heal you of your wounds,' says the Lord, 'Because they have called you an outcast saying: "This *is* Zion; No one seeks her."'

DAY 4

A little "no" never hurt nobody (or at least it shouldn't have). It's when people don't respect it that problems occur. When you stand up for how you feel about your decisions, it is easier for you to stand by your choices with confidence.

Today, I said no to:

_____

_____

_____

_____

_____

Why did I say no?

_____

_____

_____

_____

_____

Saying no made me feel:

- o   Independent
- o   Strong
- o   Guilty
- o   Mean
- o   Happy
- o   Empowered
- o   _____

My no gave me more:

- ○ Time
- ○ Opportunity
- ○ Satisfaction
- ○ Power
- ○ Anxiety

I am now available to say yes to or to do:

_____

_____

_____

_____

_____

PRAYER

I have reasons for my choices. I don't need to apologize or explain them unless it is absolutely necessary. I trust You will protect me from those who despise my stance and show them the truth on my behalf. Thank You, in Jesus' name. Amen.

Psalms 91:10 (NKJV)

No evil shall befall you, nor shall any plague come near your dwelling...

DAY 5

The journey of a seemingly pessimistic no leads toward the doorway of an optimistic yes!

Today, I said no to:

_____

_____

_____

_____

_____

Why did I say no?

_____

_____

_____

_____

_____

Saying no made me feel:

- o Independent
- o Strong
- o Guilty
- o Mean
- o Happy
- o Empowered
- o _____

My no gave me more:

- Time
- Opportunity
- Satisfaction
- Power
- Anxiety

I am now available to say yes to or to do:

_____

_____

_____

_____

_____

Prayer

Remove the guilt and shame that I feel when I stand my ground. Help me to look toward You and see positive outcomes confident that I have made the right decision with Your guidance and not my own understanding. My goal should always be to please You and not others. No one is before You. Thank You, Lord. In Jesus' name. Amen.

Psalms 91:16 (NKJV)

With long life I will satisfy him and show him My salvation.

DAY 6

Trying to convince people that your no isn't about stifling their potential but accelerating their growth isn't easy, but you don't have to.

Today, I said no to

_____

_____

_____

_____

_____

Why did I say no?

_____

_____

_____

_____

_____

Saying no made me feel:

- o Independent
- o Strong
- o Guilty
- o Mean
- o Happy
- o Empowered
- o _____

My no gave me more:

- ○ Time
- ○ Opportunity
- ○ Satisfaction
- ○ Power
- ○ Anxiety

I am now available to say yes to or to do:

_____

_____

_____

_____

_____

Prayer

Lord, help me to recognize that some jobs are just for You. I cannot do everything. Everyone won't understand me or my decisions. Help me to be okay with what others think about my choices. I recognize that I do not feel strong enough to stand on my own, but You are powerful in my weakness. Keep me lifted and heal my shortcomings and wounds of guilt. Let me unselfishly give it over to You because I trust You. In Jesus' name. Amen.

Psalms 107:20 (NKJV)

He sent His word and healed them and delivered them from their destructions.

DAY 7

No is not the end of the world but the beginning of getting your new world in order. If you keep saying yes to everyone and everything else, you may not have room left for anything you want to do. Be a little selfish. Indulge in yourself for a moment. You are worth a load of yeses!

Today, I said no to:

_____

_____

_____

_____

_____

Why did I say no?

_____

_____

_____

_____

_____

Saying no made me feel:

- o   Independent
- o   Strong
- o   Guilty
- o   Mean
- o   Happy
- o   Empowered
- o   _____

My no gave me more:

- ○ Time
- ○ Opportunity
- ○ Satisfaction
- ○ Power
- ○ Anxiety

I am now available to say yes to or to do:

_____

_____

_____

_____

_____

Prayer

I am a beautiful reflection of the Lord and all His goodness and mercy. When I awake, he says I am worth. This is not the end for me, it is just the beginning. If I have breath, I have an opportunity to do and be better. I am here to give life given to me. I am here to be a recycler of good deeds. Goodness doesn't come with guilt; it comes with wisdom that builds up not destroys or tears down. Lord, give me the wisdom to do good that leads to growth and not shortcoming so my seeds can grow and not be hindered or stunted. In Jesus' name. Amen.

Psalms 118:17 (NKJV)

I shall not die, but live, and declare the works of the Lord.

DAY 8

When you discover why you feel the need to say yes to everything, you'll have a better understanding of why you should be saying no to some things. You might notice that your yes isn't even about the other person but personal unresolved issues. Honestly, it isn't about you, it's about the person on the other end of that yes. Do you both a favor and say no this time.

Today, I said no to:

_____

_____

_____

_____

_____

Why did I say no?

_____

_____

_____

_____

_____

Saying no made me feel:

- o   Independent
- o   Strong
- o   Guilty
- o   Mean
- o   Happy
- o   Empowered
- o   _____

My no gave me more:

- ○ Time
- ○ Opportunity
- ○ Satisfaction
- ○ Power
- ○ Anxiety

I am now available to say yes to or to do:

_____

_____

_____

_____

_____

Prayer

Lord, help me reflect and get a better understanding of my need to please. I am good enough for Your love because You died for me, but I am not the only one You died for. Help me remember it is not about me but allowing You to deal with Your children. You cleanse me of my sins. Each day is an opportunity for me to thank You and praise You. Let me serve as Your messenger to my family, friends, coworkers, church, and everyone else in my life. Let them see You in me. Let them trust me because of Your light that shines through me. Prick me when I get in Your way or do Your business instead of minding my own. Let me lead others to You and not to myself. In Jesus' name. Amen.

Proverbs 4:20-22 (NKJV)

My son, give attention to my words; incline your ears to my sayings. Do not let them depart your eyes; keep them in the midst of your heart; for they are life to those who find them, and health to all their flesh.

DAY 9

Sometimes people want to read more into a no than what it is. However, it really is all that it is... a simple no. You can explain it and when the receiver doesn't want to accept it, they see it as an obstacle instead of a pathway. Politely show them the path.

Today, I said no to:

_____

_____

_____

_____

_____

Why did I say no?

_____

_____

_____

_____

_____

Saying no made me feel:

- o Independent
- o Strong
- o Guilty
- o Mean
- o Happy
- o Empowered
- o _____

My no gave me more:

- ○ Time
- ○ Opportunity
- ○ Satisfaction
- ○ Power
- ○ Anxiety

I am now available to say yes to or to do:

_____

_____

_____

_____

_____

Prayer

Lord, keep my heart and mind focused on You. Help me to stop focusing on people and things. I am very much alive in You. You give me a fresh wind. You give me my why. You understand me. You validate me. I don't need others to tell me who I am or decipher my worth. You know my heart and my decisions. Thank You for helping me to do what is best. Do not let me make any moves without the input of the Holy Spirit. In Jesus' name. Amen.

Romans 8:11 (NKJV)

But if the Spirit of Him who raised Jesus from the dead dwells in you, He who raised Christ from the dead will also give life to your mortal bodies through His Spirit who dwells in you.

DAY 10

Consistency leads to good habits and wisdom. Inconsistency leads to confusion and disorganization. When you say no and then change your position it cheapens the reason for why you said no in the first place and thwarts the lesson. Let no be no and yes be yes.

Today, I said no to:

_____

_____

_____

_____

_____

Why did I say no?

_____

_____

_____

_____

_____

Saying no made me feel:

- o Independent
- o Strong
- o Guilty
- o Mean
- o Happy
- o Empowered
- o _____

My no gave me more:

- ○ Time
- ○ Opportunity
- ○ Satisfaction
- ○ Power
- ○ Anxiety

I am now available to say yes to or to do:

_____

_____

_____

_____

_____

Prayer

Help me to be consistent in my walk with You, Lord. Let me be consistent in my words. When I cannot stand firm on my own answers, help me to defer to You. I know You will help me do the right thing. In Jesus' name. Amen.

Matthew 5:37 (NKJV)

But let your 'Yes' be 'Yes' and your 'No,' 'No'. For whatever is more than these is from the evil one.

You've reached the end of Day 10. Take a moment to write your own prayer or tell how God is leading you on your NO Journey:

_____

_____

_____

_____

_____

_____

_____

_____

_____

_____

_____

_____

_____

_____

_____

_____

_____

_____

_____

_____

_____

_____

Just Getting Warmed Up

DAY 11

"No" must be a good word, it's in the bible. It should be used as a tool for goodness and not as a weapon. It is to provide strength and independence to the recipient and you.

Today, I said no to:

_____

_____

_____

_____

_____

Why did I say no?

_____

_____

_____

_____

_____

Saying no made me feel:

- o Independent
- o Strong
- o Guilty
- o Mean
- o Happy
- o Empowered
- o _____

My no gave me more:

- o Time
- o Opportunity
- o Satisfaction
- o Power
- o Anxiety

I am now available to say yes to or to do:

_____

_____

_____

_____

_____

Prayer

Let my "no" not be taken as a negative when I use it for correcting others or helping them be strong. Don't let me renege on my good intentions. Check my heart to make sure my motives are pure. You know why I do what I do. Help me to understand that my healing comes from You. Remind me that I am Yours so that I won't succumb to pressures that make me want to change my answers. Oh, Holy One, only You can heal me from my reasons and for that I give my shortcomings over to You and praise Your name. In Jesus' name. Amen.

Jeremiah 17:14 (NKJV)

Heal me, O Lord, and I shall be healed; save me, and I shall be saved, for You are my praise.

DAY 12

Saying no isn't the worst part, it's the feeling after it's said. Understanding the root of those feelings provide even more proof that no was most likely the best answer given.

Today, I said no to:

_____

_____

_____

_____

_____

Why did I say no?

_____

_____

_____

_____

_____

Saying no made me feel:

- o Independent
- o Strong
- o Guilty
- o Mean
- o Happy
- o Empowered
- o _____

My no gave me more:

- ○ Time
- ○ Opportunity
- ○ Satisfaction
- ○ Power
- ○ Anxiety

I am now available to say yes to or to do:

_____

_____

_____

_____

_____

Prayer

It's difficult for me to say no to my loved ones. I am worried they will be upset or something scary will happen to them because of me. My stomach is in knots over these issues and my body grows weary. But You, Lord, are my strength. I know You will get me through these times. I know You will protect all that I love. I know we were Yours from the beginning and You know what is best even when we don't understand. Soothe my spirit, Oh God. It is not about me, and I am not alone in this. This was the right thing to do. Ease my mind and protect me from torturing myself. In Jesus' name. Amen.

Psalm 23:4 (ESV)

Even though I walk through the valley of the shadow of death, I will fear no evil, for you are with me; your rod and your staff, they comfort me.

DAY 13

Sometimes no is about reclaiming your own independence not making more people dependent. There are other ways of getting things done, you don't always have to be the only way.

Today, I said no to:

_____

_____

_____

_____

_____

Why did I say no?

_____

_____

_____

_____

_____

Saying no made me feel:

- o Independent
- o Strong
- o Guilty
- o Mean
- o Happy
- o Empowered
- o _____

My no gave me more:

- o Time
- o Opportunity
- o Satisfaction
- o Power
- o Anxiety

I am now available to say yes to or to do:

_____

_____

_____

_____

_____

Prayer

No one will ever fully understand the way You do, Lord. We are Your children, and You decide what is best for us. You make a way out of no way. I can only make a way out of some way and my way isn't always right. When I trust Your way and follow Your guidance, I am confident in my decisions and the outcome. It is because You lead to paths that bring life and not destruction and in that I am comforted. Thank You for Your way. In Jesus' name. Amen.

John 14:27 (NKJV)

Peace I leave with you; My peace I give to you; not as the world gives do I give to you. Let not your heart be troubled, neither let it be afraid.

DAY 14

Saying no is not the end of a problem but the beginning of a solution. It opens the door to conversations of why.

Today, I said no to:

_____

_____

_____

_____

_____

Why did I say no?

_____

_____

_____

_____

_____

Saying no made me feel:

- o Independent
- o Strong
- o Guilty
- o Mean
- o Happy
- o Empowered
- o _____

My no gave me more:

- Time
- Opportunity
- Satisfaction
- Power
- Anxiety

I am now available to say yes to or to do:

_____

_____

_____

_____

_____

Prayer

Bring peace upon my household, my family, friends, and workplace. Lord, please don't let my answer of no be a conversation stopper but a starter. Help me find ways to make my loved ones more independent and considerate. I don't want them to think I am being mean, but I do want them to understand that I cannot do everything for them. In Jesus' name. Amen.

Ephesians 4:15 (NIV)

Instead, speaking the truth in love, we will grow to become in every respect the mature body of him who is the head, that is, Christ.

DAY 15

Be sure you know the meaning of your purpose before someone tries to define it for you. God has big plans for you, seek him for the blueprint to your life not man.

Today, I said no to:

_____

_____

_____

_____

_____

Why did I say no?

_____

_____

_____

_____

_____

Saying no made me feel:

- o   Independent
- o   Strong
- o   Guilty
- o   Mean
- o   Happy
- o   Empowered
- o   _____

My no gave me more:

- ○ Time
- ○ Opportunity
- ○ Satisfaction
- ○ Power
- ○ Anxiety

I am now available to say yes to or to do:

_____

_____

_____

_____

_____

Prayer

Lord, help me figure out who I am and the true extent of my purpose. I've spent too much time allowing others to dictate aspects of my life that are reserved for You. Help me to cancel out the noise and only hear what my Father says about me and my future. In Jesus' name. Amen.

Jeremiah 29:11 (NIV)

"For I know the plans I have for you," declares the Lord, "plans to prosper you and not to harm you, plans to give you hope and a future."

DAY 16

When the world is dark and closing in around you, look to the light! God got you!

Today, I said no to:

_____

_____

_____

_____

_____

Why did I say no?

_____

_____

_____

_____

_____

Saying no made me feel:

- o Independent
- o Strong
- o Guilty
- o Mean
- o Happy
- o Empowered
- o _____

My no gave me more:

- ○ Time
- ○ Opportunity
- ○ Satisfaction
- ○ Power
- ○ Anxiety

I am now available to say yes to or to do:

_____

_____

_____

_____

_____

Prayer

Be with me when I feel weak in my spirit. When I can't muster the strength to stand on my own. When it feels like the walls are closing in, I feel You standing in the gap and not allowing the worries of life to cave in on me. Thank You for never leaving me alone and giving me the will to move on. In Jesus' name. Amen.

2 Timothy 4:22 (ESV)

The Lord be with your spirit. Grace be with you.

DAY 17

Pride is a close relative of regret. It stops love from being made. It stops forgiveness from being given. It is a selfish version of "all about me and how I feel" instead of the selfless version of what the truth really is. Swallow pride so love can live.

Today, I said no to:

_____

_____

_____

_____

_____

Why did I say no?

_____

_____

_____

_____

_____

Saying no made me feel:

- o   Independent
- o   Strong
- o   Guilty
- o   Mean
- o   Happy
- o   Empowered
- o   _____

My no gave me more:

- ○ Time
- ○ Opportunity
- ○ Satisfaction
- ○ Power
- ○ Anxiety

I am now available to say yes to or to do:

_____

_____

_____

_____

_____

Prayer

I cannot do this life alone. When my pride gets in the way and I begin to say yes to something I should refuse, take over, Holy Spirit. I cannot do everything. There are others who are more talented or may have more time to do the work. Help me to move out of the way of God and step into the purpose of God. In Jesus' name. Amen.

Romans 8:26 (ESV)

Likewise, the Spirit helps us in our weakness. For we do not know what to pray for as we ought, but the Spirit himself intercedes for us with groanings too deep for words.

DAY 18

Fear has no place here. Do it afraid and do it again. You are able, capable, more than enough, an abundance and overflow of the awesomeness of God's greatest gift!

Today, I said no to:

_____

_____

_____

_____

_____

Why did I say no?

_____

_____

_____

_____

_____

Saying no made me feel:

- o   Independent
- o   Strong
- o   Guilty
- o   Mean
- o   Happy
- o   Empowered
- o   _____

My no gave me more:

- o   Time
- o   Opportunity
- o   Satisfaction
- o   Power
- o   Anxiety

I am now available to say yes to or to do:

_____

_____

_____

_____

_____

Prayer

God, You waste nothing including me. You use every bit of my purpose. You recycle me like soil in the earth. You give me the courage and talents to return onto You double what You have given, so I can accomplish even greater things. I am not afraid to step out on faith and accomplish the goals set before me because I know that You are near. In Jesus' name. Amen.

Deuteronomy 31:6 (NIV)

Be strong and courageous. Do not be afraid or terrified because of them, for the Lord your God goes with you; he will never leave you nor forsake you.

DAY 19

The kids of today aren't like the kids of yesterday. They are the future of tomorrow! They are hungry and they are ready. Our responsibility is to feed them. We got time in the game and wisdom on our side because they aren't slowing down for nothing. We must be intentional, diligent, and consistent. We must be ready, too. They lead the future, but we guide it!

Today, I said no to:

_____

_____

_____

_____

_____

Why did I say no?

_____

_____

_____

_____

_____

Saying no made me feel:

- o Independent
- o Strong
- o Guilty
- o Mean
- o Happy
- o Empowered
- o _____

My no gave me more:

- ○ Time
- ○ Opportunity
- ○ Satisfaction
- ○ Power
- ○ Anxiety

I am now available to say yes to or to do:

_____

_____

_____

_____

_____

Prayer

I want to change my answer so many times when I look into the adorable faces of the ones I love but consistency is what helps them to stay on task and it will help them in the future. Help me trust that I do what is best for them, so I don't change my mind. They may not understand my reasoning now but one day they will. I trust You even when I cannot trust myself. I know You know what is best for us and I am for sure about Your love. Let them be for sure about my love, correction, and direction. In Jesus' name. Amen.

Jeremiah 17:7 (NIV)

But blessed is the one who trusts in the Lord, whose confidence is in him.

DAY 20

The past cannot exist in the present. This is why there is so much tension when it tries to come up. You just must let go of some things. If the past is not coming up for your benefit or the benefit of others, it will crush you. Yesterday is in direct conflict with today and today will never catch tomorrow. The past plants, the present trends, and the future reaps. Go forward!

Today, I said no to:

_____

_____

_____

_____

_____

Why did I say no?

_____

_____

_____

_____

_____

Saying no made me feel:

- o Independent
- o Strong
- o Guilty
- o Mean
- o Happy
- o Empowered
- o _____

My no gave me more:

- ○ Time
- ○ Opportunity
- ○ Satisfaction
- ○ Power
- ○ Anxiety

I am now available to say yes to or to do:

_____

_____

_____

_____

_____

Prayer

I pray You allow me to reap all the benefits of a well planted past, healthy present, and bountiful future! Help me to see pass the past and into a beautiful future awaiting. My past has me feeling so guilty sometimes and I try to compensate at my own expense. Help me accept my past and use it as a steppingstone and not a stumbling block. In Jesus' name. Amen.

2 Corinthians 5:17 (ESV)
Therefore, if anyone is in Christ, he is a new creation. The old has passed away; behold, the new has come.

You've reached the end of Day 20. Take a moment to write your own prayer or tell how God is leading you on your NO Journey:

_____

_____

_____

_____

_____

_____

_____

_____

_____

_____

_____

_____

_____

_____

_____

_____

_____

_____

_____

_____

_____

This Isn't So Bad

DAY 21

It's in the quietness that we get our most profound answers. This time and space of nothingness is where the most life happens. The stillness of our thoughts, our reckoning and resolve. The moment of peace where we hush our thoughts and demand our brains to just let us just stop thinking for the moment and just listen.

Today, I said no to:

_____

_____

_____

_____

_____

Why did I say no?

_____

_____

_____

_____

_____

Saying no made me feel:

- o   Independent
- o   Strong
- o   Guilty
- o   Mean
- o   Happy
- o   Empowered
- o   _____

My no gave me more:

- ○ Time
- ○ Opportunity
- ○ Satisfaction
- ○ Power
- ○ Anxiety

I am now available to say yes to or to do:

_____

_____

_____

_____

_____

Prayer

Lord, speak to me? What is it You want me to know? Where is it You want me to go. Light the path I am to follow. Make Your steps plain before me. Quiet my inner turmoil. Protect me from my enemies so that You can rejuvenate me for the battle, show me the battle plan and equip me with the artillery to win this thing. Remove the distractions of my mind. Quiet what they said. Quiet what happened this morning. Quiet what I plan to do next. Quiet what I will say the next time. Quiet who I should speak to about this. Quiet everything in me that is desiring to speak up and out or even respond at all. Open me up to listen for Your voice in the still and obey. In Jesus' name. Amen

1 Samuel 3:10 (NIV)

The LORD came and stood there, calling as at the other times, "Samuel! Samuel!" Then Samuel said, "Speak, for your servant is listening."

DAY 22

When giants come up in your life, what is your rock and sling shot? What is your weapon of choice? Who do you call upon? Do you call upon the Lord like David or do you rely on yourself or someone else?

Today, I said no to:

_____

_____

_____

_____

_____

Why did I say no?

_____

_____

_____

_____

_____

Saying no made me feel:

- o Independent
- o Strong
- o Guilty
- o Mean
- o Happy
- o Empowered
- o _____

My no gave me more:

- ○ Time
- ○ Opportunity
- ○ Satisfaction
- ○ Power
- ○ Anxiety

I am now available to say yes to or to do:

_____

_____

_____

_____

_____

Prayer

Precious and Mighty Father, I cannot fight this battle on my own. I call upon You. Holy Spirit be the force that propels my weapon forward against the attack of the enemy and strike him with a fatal blow! In Your name, if David can slay a lion and bear with his bare hands and Samson a thousand men with a donkey's jawbone and not break in the process, surely, I can withstand this trial and come out standing victoriously. You are with me and that is enough. Let me move and act on Your call and not my own. I was made for this time, and You have equipped me for battle. Lord, go before me. Your mighty name is my war cry before I march forward in victory! In Jesus' name. Amen.

Judges 15:16 (NIV)

Then Samson said, "With a donkey's jawbone I have made donkeys of them. With a donkey's jawbone I have killed a thousand men."

DAY 23

You are worthy. More than enough. Bigger than ever expected or deserved. Far more than ever imagined. You mean something!

Today, I said no to:

_____

_____

_____

_____

_____

Why did I say no?

_____

_____

_____

_____

_____

Saying no made me feel:

- o Independent
- o Strong
- o Guilty
- o Mean
- o Happy
- o Empowered
- o _____

My no gave me more:

- Time
- Opportunity
- Satisfaction
- Power
- Anxiety

I am now available to say yes to or to do:

_____

_____

_____

_____

_____

Prayer

God, You waste nothing including me. You use every bit of my purpose. You recycle me like soil in the earth. You give me the courage and talents to return onto You double what You have given, so I can accomplish even greater things. I am not afraid to step out on faith and accomplish the goals set before me because I know that You are near. In Jesus' name. Amen.

Joshua 1:6 (NIV)

Be strong and courageous, because you will lead these people to inherit the land I swore to their ancestors to give them.

DAY 24

New day, new opportunity, new chance to do it better than ever! Where there was no strength, may you find yourself getting stronger. You have more power than you even know! What a good day!

Today, I said no to:

_____
_____
_____
_____
_____

Why did I say no?

_____
_____
_____
_____
_____

Saying no made me feel:

- o Independent
- o Strong
- o Guilty
- o Mean
- o Happy
- o Empowered
- o _____

My no gave me more:

- ○ Time
- ○ Opportunity
- ○ Satisfaction
- ○ Power
- ○ Anxiety

I am now available to say yes to or to do:

_____

_____

_____

_____

_____

Prayer

Lord, You are my source of strength. You define my days and my nights. I am in control because You are in control of me. I am powerful because You are powerful in me. Even at my weakest, You are strong. Give me the power to reclaim what is mine whether it is time, energy, or resources. Thank You for having it all and blessing me with it. This is Your day that You have blessed me to be a part of and I will spend it praising Your name and giving You the glory. In Jesus' name. Amen.

Psalm 118:24 (ESV)

This is the day the Lord has made; let us rejoice and be glad in it.

DAY 25

When it seems like there is nothing else to cling to, grab hold of hope and don't let go. You can't control people, how they think or what they do but you can control you. In the hardest and happiest of times, hope will be there. Treasure it. Use it up. It never runs out, just like God's love for you. Hope is a fountain overflowing!

Today, I said no to:

_____

_____

_____

_____

_____

Why did I say no?

_____

_____

_____

_____

_____

Saying no made me feel:

- o   Independent
- o   Strong
- o   Guilty
- o   Mean
- o   Happy
- o   Empowered
- o   _____

My no gave me more:

- o Time
- o Opportunity
- o Satisfaction
- o Power
- o Anxiety

I am now available to say yes to or to do:

_____

_____

_____

_____

_____

Prayer

Almighty God, You just keep blessing me with abundance and overflow. Every time I think I have too much You show me more ways to give. When I don't feel I have enough, You give me more than I could've imagined. Thank You for the way You keep loving me. I cannot find in others or in things what I find in You. Your agape love overwhelms my soul, and I am just in awe of Your goodness. Thank You for the overflow because You know exactly what I need. In Jesus' name. Amen.

Ephesians 3:17-19 (NIV)

So that Christ may dwell in your hearts through faith. And I pray that you, being rooted and established in love, may have power, together with all the Lord's holy people, to grasp how wide and long and high and deep is the love of Christ, and to know this love that surpasses knowledge—that you may be filled to the measure of all the fullness of God.

DAY 26

Yep, it can be lonely at the top...if you let it. Bring people with you, pour into your "crowd", and don't be afraid to hang out with some other mountain toppers. Basically, make room in your space for others by building useful relationships. After all, the Word says, it's not good for us to be alone. So, who's in your crowd? Who are you building up? Who are you taking with you?

Today, I said no to:

_____

_____

_____

_____

_____

Why did I say no?

_____

_____

_____

_____

_____

Saying no made me feel:

- o Independent
- o Strong
- o Guilty
- o Mean
- o Happy
- o Empowered
- o _____

My no gave me more:

- ○ Time
- ○ Opportunity
- ○ Satisfaction
- ○ Power
- ○ Anxiety

I am now available to say yes to or to do:

_____

_____

_____

_____

_____

Prayer

Lord, I want to be in relationship with others but for all the right reasons and none of the wrong. I believe we all can do better when we work together. I don't need a bunch of yes people around me. Bless me with friends who aren't afraid to push back or tell me no because they love me. Surround me with people who don't take my no personally and understand that I want what is best for them and their future. Search my heart and guide my yes and no, Lord, so I can make good decisions. In Jesus' name. Amen.

Ecclesiastes 4:9-10 (NIV)

Two are better than one, because they have a good return for their labor: If either of them falls down, one can help the other up. But pity anyone who falls and has no one to help them up.

DAY 27

Practice saying no quickly and yes slowly to people who want an immediate answer. The best way to do this is by saying, "Unless you give me a particular time to decide, I am going to have to say no for now until I can think it through." "Maybe" gives too much hope and if you change it to "no" later there may be disappointment because of expectation.

Today, I said no to:

_____

_____

_____

_____

_____

Why did I say no?

_____

_____

_____

_____

_____

Saying no made me feel:

- o Independent
- o Strong
- o Guilty
- o Mean
- o Happy
- o Empowered
- o _____

My no gave me more:

- Time
- Opportunity
- Satisfaction
- Power
- Anxiety

I am now available to say yes to or to do:

_____

_____

_____

_____

_____

Prayer

Lord, give me the strength to be obedient in following the path You have set before me. Let my ears hear Your voice clearly so I only move in Your direction and not my own. Be the light in my life way so I can see Your hands pointing me in the way I should go. There are times when I get so caught up in what others are saying or how they are feeling that I do what pleases them instead of what is pleasing to You. Light the way for me, O God. Turn my head toward You and what You want and what You say. Let me look to please You. I know You won't let me put myself, my family, or my finances in harm's way. Help me hear Your voice over the noise of life. In Jesus' name. Amen.

John 10:27-28 (KJV)

My sheep hear my voice, and I know them, and they follow me: And I give unto them eternal life; and they shall never perish, neither shall any man pluck them out of my hand.

DAY 28

Stop locking yourself into a cell with the key in your hand. You are free! You can go! Stop letting chains with no locks and strings with no ties hold you down. Get up and walk! You are free! Go out and do! You are free! Step forward and be! You are FREE! Slave to none, Master of Self! You are free!

Today, I said no to:

_____

_____

_____

_____

_____

Why did I say no?

_____

_____

_____

_____

_____

Saying no made me feel:

- o   Independent
- o   Strong
- o   Guilty
- o   Mean
- o   Happy
- o   Empowered
- o   _____

My no gave me more:

- ○ Time
- ○ Opportunity
- ○ Satisfaction
- ○ Power
- ○ Anxiety

I am now available to say yes to or to do:

_____

_____

_____

_____

_____

Prayer

Lord, help me to remove self-sabotage, self-harm, and self-hate from my life. Help me to stop criticizing myself and understand that when I do this, I am criticizing Your creation. You give me life. You have set me free from my past, from my sins, and from my burdens. Don't let me go locking myself into a cell after You have given me the keys to freedom. I am free and I deserve this freedom because You feel I was enough. Help my heart, mind, and actions get in alignment with the truth and never imprison myself, again. You've granted me freedom. I am worthy. In Jesus' name. Amen.

John 8:36 (NIV)

So if the Son sets free, you will be free indeed.

DAY 29

Sometimes a good no is the only thing that keeps it all together because of its shock value. People aren't used to it, they don't like it, and they don't want to hear it again. Maybe they'll do the right thing the next time just to hear you say yes, again.

Today, I said no to:

_____
_____
_____
_____
_____

Why did I say no?

_____
_____
_____
_____
_____

Saying no made me feel:

- o Independent
- o Strong
- o Guilty
- o Mean
- o Happy
- o Empowered
- o _____

My no gave me more:

- Time
- Opportunity
- Satisfaction
- Power
- Anxiety

I am now available to say yes to or to do:

_____
_____
_____
_____
_____

Prayer

Lord, I love You!!! I want to thank You for every thistle and every thorn. They make me sharper! Every bump and every bruise. They make me tougher! Every put down and every let down. They make me stronger! Thank You for every heartache and heart break. They make me yearn to love more! Everything is for my good, even when it doesn't seem like it. Everything is for Your purpose in me and of me and it is good. I will get through because You are in me and with me. I will rise and rise, again, because You are the source of my strength. I know that I will love and love, again, because You give me the capacity to love more. I can love more because You, Almighty God, love more! You first loved me! You are love and I am nothing without You, so thank You, again and forever! In Jesus' name. Amen.

Colossians 1:17 (ESV)

And he is before all things, and in him all things hold together.

DAY 30

It seems like "yes" has all the fun during the harvest. However, when it comes time for the reaping season, you really see the true benefit of the "no". Good things come through patience but anxious decisions breed regret.

Today, I said no to:

_____

_____

_____

_____

_____

Why did I say no?

_____

_____

_____

_____

_____

Saying no made me feel:

- o   Independent
- o   Strong
- o   Guilty
- o   Mean
- o   Happy
- o   Empowered
- o   _____

My no gave me more:

- Time
- Opportunity
- Satisfaction
- Power
- Anxiety

I am now available to say yes to or to do:

_____

_____

_____

_____

_____

Prayer

Lord, I know I am on the brink of something awesome. I submit all my plans to You. I wait with patience and joy. I wait with love and kindness. I wait with boldness and determination. I wait in anticipation of what's to come. I wait with excitement of what's to come! Promises fulfilled! Hope realized. Greatness recognized. Glory magnified! I give my all to You, Lord. I lay it at Your feet with an open heart. Emptied, poured out, nothing left for anything but You! I am Your vessel! Fill me with Your abundant love, Almighty God. In Jesus' name. Amen.

Proverbs 16:3 (ESV)

Commit your work to the Lord, and your plans will be established.

You've reached the end of Day 30. Take a moment to write your own prayer or tell how God is leading you on your NO Journey:

_____

_____

_____

_____

_____

_____

_____

_____

_____

_____

_____

_____

_____

_____

_____

_____

_____

_____

_____

_____

_____

You Can Do This

DAY 31

You have just as much a right to say no as you do to say yes. Just like people love and respect when you say yes, they must also respect and love when you say no. Thank goodness for rights!

Today, I said no to:

_____

_____

_____

_____

_____

Why did I say no?

_____

_____

_____

_____

_____

Saying no made me feel:

- o Independent
- o Strong
- o Guilty
- o Mean
- o Happy
- o Empowered
- o _____

My no gave me more:

- ○ Time
- ○ Opportunity
- ○ Satisfaction
- ○ Power
- ○ Anxiety

I am now available to say yes to or to do:

_____

_____

_____

_____

_____

Prayer

Thank You so much for the ability to do things that we take for granted every day. Thank You for the ability to talk, walk, move, breathe, hear, see, taste, touch, feel, believe, disbelieve, hurt, express, want, need, desire, and love. Thank You for first times, last times, times again, lifetimes, and second chances. Thank You for every I love You; I need You, and I forgive You and will You forgive me, and thank You for forgiving me. Thank You for being able to decide, choose, say no, and say yes. Thank You for the ability to be undecided, say maybe or maybe not, and say yes or no, or I don't think so or I don't know. Thank You for the ability to make a choice, to think, to know, to seek, to understand, to shut down, to charge forward, to hold back, to give more, to keep going or to stand still. Thank You for so many things that we take for granted every day like the ability to move our hands, to move our mouth, to speak and have a voice and words to come out. Thank You for the ability to speak our displeasure and to share what we love and explain the things that we don't like but also the things that we do. Thank You for the ability to even live. Thank You for loved ones and thank You for relatives and friends. Thank You for everything because all things come from You. Lord, we treasure You, appreciate You, and thank You for giving us so much love, grace, and mercy. Thank You for coming here and living among us. Thank You for being so compassionate and so loving and understanding although sometimes we don't even understand or love ourselves enough. Thank You for thinking enough of us. Thank You for loving us enough. Thank You for everything and all things. In Jesus' name. Amen.

2 Timothy 1:7 (NIV)

For the Spirit God gave us does not make us timid, but gives us power, love, and self-discipline.

I was told I should fill this page with something, but I said, "No." Proceed...

DAY 32

Reminder to family: "No" does not mean I don't love you. We may not agree on every issue but that doesn't give us a reason to not love each other. This time I am agreeing with myself and sticking by my decision and hoping it will be okay for all of us.

Today, I said no to:

_____

_____

_____

_____

_____

Why did I say no?

_____

_____

_____

_____

_____

Saying no made me feel:

- o   Independent
- o   Strong
- o   Guilty
- o   Mean
- o   Happy
- o   Empowered
- o   _____

My no gave me more:

- o Time
- o Opportunity
- o Satisfaction
- o Power
- o Anxiety

I am now available to say yes to or to do:

_____

_____

_____

_____

_____

Prayer

Let my loved ones see how much I love them by my heart and intentions. Help me to be okay even if they do get upset with my decision to say no. Help me to be okay standing my ground and not second guess my decision or feel bad about it. Allow love to move freely within my family. Close gaps and tie up loose ends. Help me to open my heart to forgiving others and soften any hardened hearts towards me. Only You know what tomorrow will bring, let us rejoice in today. In Jesus' name. Amen.

1 John 3:18 (NIV)

Dear children, let us not love with words or speech but with actions and in truth.

DAY 33

The young feel as if they are racing the clock. However, it isn't the clock of time but the clock of purpose! Our sacrifices and let downs may lead us into some unexpected places but every no is just a doorway to other possibilities. Possibilities lead to opportunities and opportunities lead right to PURPOSE!

Today, I said no to:

_____

_____

_____

_____

_____

Why did I say no?

_____

_____

_____

_____

Saying no made me feel:

- o Independent
- o Strong
- o Guilty
- o Mean
- o Happy
- o Empowered
- o _____

My no gave me more:

- ○ Time
- ○ Opportunity
- ○ Satisfaction
- ○ Power
- ○ Anxiety

I am now available to say yes to or to do:

_____

_____

_____

_____

_____

Prayer

Lord, I'll admit that I hate hearing the word no and that's why I have such a time saying it. Is my no going to block or deny someone entry? Is my no going to create a negative impact on my job, family, community, or education? Help me to be confident that my no isn't in vain, malice, or anger. My no is a door opener and every no I experience places me in direct proximity of my future, whether I like it or not. Lord, You are good and no can be as good as yes. Though "no" can feel like punishment when we don't get our way or understand, help us to see the lesson and the good in it. In Jesus' name. Amen.

Job 13:15 (NKJV)

Though He slay me, yet will I trust Him. Even so, I will defend my own ways before Him.

DAY 34

It may seem scary to believe in yourself or even scarier to trust in others but the biggest thing to fear is a disbelief in the one who created it all. If you can't find hope in anything else; you most certainly can find it in Jesus! He's the one that can make something from nothing. Hopes, dreams, ideas, and people.

Today, I said no to:

_____

_____

_____

_____

_____

Why did I say no?

_____

_____

_____

_____

_____

Saying no made me feel:

- ○ Independent
- ○ Strong
- ○ Guilty
- ○ Mean
- ○ Happy
- ○ Empowered
- ○ _____

My no gave me more:

- ○ Time
- ○ Opportunity
- ○ Satisfaction
- ○ Power
- ○ Anxiety

I am now available to say yes to or to do:

_____

_____

_____

_____

_____

Prayer

Lord, You are the only one who can turn misery into ministry; mistakes into miracles; the unlikely into the most likely, and loss into victory. You are awesome and You are able! Thank You for sustaining me and giving me an abundance. I honor You! Thank You, Father! In Jesus' name. Amen.

Psalms 33:18-19 (NIV)

But the eyes of the LORD are on those who fear him, on those whose hope is in his unfailing love, to deliver them from death and keep them alive in famine.

DAY 35

Our children show us the best and worst of ourselves. Sometimes when we fuss at them, we are convicted of our own shortcomings, not to make us stop teaching them but to make us own up to our own mess and do better for the next generation.

Today, I said no to:

_____

_____

_____

_____

_____

Why did I say no?

_____

_____

_____

_____

_____

Saying no made me feel:

- ○ Independent
- ○ Strong
- ○ Guilty
- ○ Mean
- ○ Happy
- ○ Empowered
- ○ _____

My no gave me more:

- Time
- Opportunity
- Satisfaction
- Power
- Anxiety

I am now available to say yes to or to do:

_____

_____

_____

_____

_____

Prayer

Let me leave an awesome legacy for my family, friends, and community and when I look at my offspring help me see the best and better version of myself and strive even harder to be that! In Jesus' name. Amen.

Psalm 112:1-3 (ESV)

Praise the LORD! Blessed is the man who fears the LORD, who greatly delights in his commandments! His offspring will be mighty in the land; the generation of the upright will be blessed. Wealth and riches are in his house, and his righteousness endures forever.

DAY 36

Be mindful to treat others well especially when they don't have, so they remember your kindness when they do. That doesn't mean you have to say yes to their every request, but it does mean that you should help as much as you can without putting a burden on yourself.

Today, I said no to:

_____

_____

_____

_____

_____

Why did I say no?

_____

_____

_____

_____

_____

Saying no made me feel:

- o Independent
- o Strong
- o Guilty
- o Mean
- o Happy
- o Empowered
- o _____

My no gave me more:

- ○ Time
- ○ Opportunity
- ○ Satisfaction
- ○ Power
- ○ Anxiety

I am now available to say yes to or to do:

_____

_____

_____

_____

_____

Prayer

Help me to treat others how I want to be treated. Let me give with goodness in mind. Don't let me get upset or resentful at what I have given or how much because it shouldn't be a burden to me. I know whatever I give belongs to the Lord. He will replenish and replace everything that is missing or empty from my life. In Jesus' name. Amen.

Matthew 7:12 (NIV)

So, in everything, do to others what you would have them do to you, for this sums up the Law and the Prophets.

DAY 37

Breakthrough happens when it is supposed to, not a moment before or after. Breakthrough happens right on time. Be patient and wait for it. Don't change your no, change your mindset. Be patient and see it is worth it.

Today, I said no to:

_____

_____

_____

_____

_____

Why did I say no?

_____

_____

_____

_____

_____

Saying no made me feel:

- o Independent
- o Strong
- o Guilty
- o Mean
- o Happy
- o Empowered
- o _____

My no gave me more:

- Time
- Opportunity
- Satisfaction
- Power
- Anxiety

I am now available to say yes to or to do:

_____

_____

_____

_____

_____

Prayer

Lord, I am joyously awaiting my breakthrough. You see me through all times. I will not look at my down moments with sadness although they can sting. You said in Your word that all things are working together for my good and I am excited. I will continue to do good in Your sight. I will continue to pray for family and friends and even my enemies. You know what is best for me. You do what is in my best interest and I trust You. Although I am excited, I will wait patiently on You. In Jesus' name. Amen.

Ecclesiastes 7:8 (NIV)

The end of a matter is better than its beginning, and patience is better than pride.

DAY 38

Some things can be reconciled in your mind and heart before it even passes through your lips. Think it out before you speak it out loud.

Today, I said no to:

_____

_____

_____

_____

_____

Why did I say no?

_____

_____

_____

_____

_____

Saying no made me feel:

- ○ Independent
- ○ Strong
- ○ Guilty
- ○ Mean
- ○ Happy
- ○ Empowered
- ○ _____

My no gave me more:

- ○ Time
- ○ Opportunity
- ○ Satisfaction
- ○ Power
- ○ Anxiety

I am now available to say yes to or to do:

_____

_____

_____

_____

_____

Prayer

Help me to think before I speak. Let me think about the consequences. Let me think about the lasting impact it will make on every ear that may hear it. Let me weigh the cost carefully and decide if the words are worth it. Don't let pride or tempers let the words spill or fear convince them to stay. Let me be sure and in control of what I say and who I say it to. In Jesus' name. Amen.

Proverbs 21:23 (NIV)

Those who guard their mouths, and their tongues keep themselves from calamity.

DAY 39

The world will have you believing lies about yourself, but the world didn't give you your life, purpose, or gifts. God did. He gave you everything you need to walk in what He destined your impact to be. It was in you all the time and it doesn't take the world to see it, just you to believe it.

Today, I said no to:

_____

_____

_____

_____

_____

Why did I say no?

_____

_____

_____

_____

Saying no made me feel:

- o Independent
- o Strong
- o Guilty
- o Mean
- o Happy
- o Empowered
- o _____

My no gave me more:

- ○ Time
- ○ Opportunity
- ○ Satisfaction
- ○ Power
- ○ Anxiety

I am now available to say yes to or to do:

_____

_____

_____

_____

_____

Prayer

I was born with purpose. You gave me a destiny before my parents even knew of my conception. You had a plan for me set out. Fill me with confidence in You so that I can trust what I hear You saying to me. In Your word You say that I am good. You say I am precious in Your sight. It doesn't matter what the world says about me. It matters what You think about me. The world will love me for a moment and hate me the next, but You are consistent, You love me always. You want what is best for me and I choose to believe You. In Jesus' name. Amen.

John 15:18-19 (NKJV)

"If the world hates you, you know that it hated Me before it hated you. If you were of the world, the world would love its own. Yet because you are not of the world, but I chose you out of the world, therefore the world hates you."

DAY 40

When you come to God, wholeheartedly, broken, weak, confused, scared, hurt, tired or even with your good times, He listens. He picks up the pieces and puts them back together with no cracks. Stop taking people's pieces, show them the peacemaker. Only He can make all of us whole by filling our holes.

Today, I said no to:

_____

_____

_____

_____

_____

Why did I say no?

_____

_____

_____

_____

_____

Saying no made me feel:

- o Independent
- o Strong
- o Guilty
- o Mean
- o Happy
- o Empowered
- o _____

My no gave me more:

- Time
- Opportunity
- Satisfaction
- Power
- Anxiety

I am now available to say yes to or to do:

_____

_____

_____

_____

_____

Prayer

Only You can pick up the pieces in my life and make me whole again. Forgive me for trying to patch myself together without You. Forgive me for trying to take on the problems of others without Your help. My children were Your children before they were mine. My job was Yours before it was mine. My loved ones belonged to You first. Excuse me for stepping out of line. Help me to give You everything and wait on Your direction before I make any decision. I've decided that a lot of these issues were too much for me in the very beginning and I had no business in it. I am stepping back in my place, so You can do what You do to restore and redeem. In Jesus' name. Amen.

1 Peter 5:10 (NIV)

And the God of all grace, who called you to his eternal glory in Christ, after you have suffered a little while, will himself restore you and make you strong, firm, and steadfast.

You've reached the end of Day 40. Take a moment to write your own prayer or tell how God is leading you on your NO Journey:

_____

_____

_____

_____

_____

_____

_____

_____

_____

_____

_____

_____

_____

_____

_____

_____

_____

_____

_____

_____

_____

Keep Up the Good Work

DAY 41

Sprinkle a little "no" around like salt and let it add some flavor to your life. If you get used to it, you'll discover it wasn't so bad after all.

Today, I said no to:

_____

_____

_____

_____

_____

Why did I say no?

_____

_____

_____

_____

_____

Saying no made me feel:

- o   Independent
- o   Strong
- o   Guilty
- o   Mean
- o   Happy
- o   Empowered
- o   _____

My no gave me more:

- ○ Time
- ○ Opportunity
- ○ Satisfaction
- ○ Power
- ○ Anxiety

I am now available to say yes to or to do:

_____

_____

_____

_____

_____

Prayer

Me saying no is not meant to purposely hurt anyone. I say it because it is what I feel is best for the person, the situation, or myself. I say it for a reason and not selfish ones. I say it to protect my space, self, and sanity. I say it because it is the right thing to do in the context of the situation that I am saying it in. Help me be proud of my decision and not intimidated by it. Some may not like my response, but I do, and You know how important this realization is for me. Grant me the boldness to walk in my decision. In Jesus' name. Amen.

Matthew 5:13 (NIV)

You are the salt of the earth. But if the salt loses its saltiness, how can it be made salty again? It is no longer good for anything, except to be thrown out and trampled underfoot.

DAY 42

A good "no" is better than a bad "no" any day. A good no is for a good reason, a bad no is for no good reason at all. Reclaiming your no, however, is good.

Today, I said no to:

_____

_____

_____

_____

_____

Why did I say no?

_____

_____

_____

_____

Saying no made me feel:

- o Independent
- o Strong
- o Guilty
- o Mean
- o Happy
- o Empowered
- o _____

My no gave me more:

- ○ Time
- ○ Opportunity
- ○ Satisfaction
- ○ Power
- ○ Anxiety

I am now available to say yes to or to do:

_____

_____

_____

_____

_____

Prayer

Let my no be a good no. A no that is given to empower. Lord, they need to learn to call on You on their own, not me. They need to understand that You are the reason I can say yes so many times. Let them want to know You because Your light allows me to shine. Nothing I do on my own. In Jesus' name. Amen.

Matthew 5:14–16 (NIV)

You are the light of the world. A town built on a hill cannot be hidden. Neither do people light a lamp and put it under a bowl. Instead, they put it on its stand, and it gives light to everyone in the house. In the same way, let your light shine before others, that they may see your good deeds and glorify your Father in heaven.

DAY 43

Your no should be like an unwanted Christmas gift. No take backs or regifting. Just let it sit there as a reminder to say what you really want the next time.

Today, I said no to:

_____
_____
_____
_____
_____

Why did I say no?

_____
_____
_____
_____
_____

Saying no made me feel:

- ○ Independent
- ○ Strong
- ○ Guilty
- ○ Mean
- ○ Happy
- ○ Empowered
- ○ _____

My no gave me more:

- ○ Time
- ○ Opportunity
- ○ Satisfaction
- ○ Power
- ○ Anxiety

I am now available to say yes to or to do:

_____

_____

_____

_____

_____

Prayer

No returns. No takebacks. Lord, You accept me as I am. I love You because with You I am enough. I don't have to try to impress You. I don't have to put on any performances to get Your love. I am awesome because You are awesome within me. You help me to be strong against the enemy because You strengthen all my areas of weakness and protect me. With You, I am always enough. You are the perfect gift! In Jesus' name. Amen.

Romans 5:17 (NIV)

For if, by the trespass of the one man, death reigned through that one man, how much more will those who receive God's abundant provision of grace and of the gift of righteousness reign in life through the one man, Jesus Christ!

DAY 44

It's hard to stand up for yourself when people keep knocking you down. However, each time you get up, it makes you that much stronger. Soon you will be able to stand your ground, and no one will be able to move you!

Today, I said no to:

_____
_____
_____
_____
_____

Why did I say no?

_____
_____
_____
_____
_____

Saying no made me feel:

- o Independent
- o Strong
- o Guilty
- o Mean
- o Happy
- o Empowered
- o _____

My no gave me more:

- o   Time
- o   Opportunity
- o   Satisfaction
- o   Power
- o   Anxiety

I am now available to say yes to or to do:

_____

_____

_____

_____

_____

Prayer

There is no one better than me. Just as I am better than no one. There is no place I do not belong. Giants go before me because You go before me, Jesus. I am powerful because of the army of angels You have surrounded me with that look out for my care. People can plot against me in private, but You hear them and direct me to safety. I love You, Lord, and I am aware of Your covering. I don't ever want to diminish the magnitude of the footprint You leave in my life. In Jesus' name. Amen.

Ephesians 6:10-11 (NIV)

Finally, be strong in the Lord and in his mighty power. Put on the full armor of God so that you can take your stand against the devil's schemes.

DAY 45

There are no resets in life. We can't go back to yesterday or hit rewind on the remote of life. We can, however, start with today.

Today, I said no to:

_____

_____

_____

_____

_____

Why did I say no?

_____

_____

_____

_____

_____

Saying no made me feel:

- o   Independent
- o   Strong
- o   Guilty
- o   Mean
- o   Happy
- o   Empowered
- o   _____

My no gave me more:

- o Time
- o Opportunity
- o Satisfaction
- o Power
- o Anxiety

I am now available to say yes to or to do:

_____

_____

_____

_____

_____

Prayer

It's a new day, Lord. Time to do it all over, again. Time to do what is right by looking ahead toward my future and not looking back at the past. I will be as new as the day and as radiant as the sunset rising! All because of You, Lord and I am grateful. In Jesus' name. Amen.

Luke 1:78-79 (GW)

A new day will dawn on us from above because our God is loving and merciful. He will give light to those who live in the dark and in death's shadow. He will guide us into the way of peace.

DAY 46

Repent, Lament, make AMENDS, find Strength to Heal, and Forgive. Forgiveness is really a two-way street! When you cross it, you must remember to look both ways!

Today, I said no to:

_____

_____

_____

_____

_____

Why did I say no?

_____

_____

_____

_____

_____

Saying no made me feel:

- ○ Independent
- ○ Strong
- ○ Guilty
- ○ Mean
- ○ Happy
- ○ Empowered
- ○ _____

My no gave me more:

- o   Time
- o   Opportunity
- o   Satisfaction
- o   Power
- o   Anxiety

I am now available to say yes to or to do:

_____

_____

_____

_____

_____

Prayer

Help me to remember that I am not perfect. I make mistakes and have rubbed people the wrong way. Let me remember that so I can be quick to say I am sorry, forgive, have mercy, repent, and lament. When I start getting self-righteous prick my heart, Holy Spirit. In Jesus' name. Amen.

Luke 17:4 (NIV)

"Even if they sin against you seven times in a day and seven times come back to you saying, 'I repent,' you must forgive them."

DAY 47

Love knows it's job very well. Let it go to work in YOU. Don't be a fool or a mat or the same as you were before. It just simply means to just let love in and in the end, it will win, whether ties loosen or ties mend, in the end love wins!

Today, I said no to:

_____

_____

_____

_____

_____

Why did I say no?

_____

_____

_____

_____

_____

Saying no made me feel:

- o Independent
- o Strong
- o Guilty
- o Mean
- o Happy
- o Empowered
- o _____

My no gave me more:

- ○ Time
- ○ Opportunity
- ○ Satisfaction
- ○ Power
- ○ Anxiety

I am now available to say yes to or to do:

_____

_____

_____

_____

_____

Prayer

Lord, Your word says love wins. You are love. You fill me with Your agape love. You love and pursue me relentlessly. I get lost in Your love. When it seems like I don't have enough in my tank to keep going because of all the evil surrounding me, You give me a reason to find new hope. Thanks for all the victories that combat all the struggles. The love that conquers all the hate. In the end You win and so love wins! In Jesus' name. Amen.

1 Peter 4:8 (GW)

Above all, show sincere love to each other, because love brings about the forgiveness of many sins.

DAY 48

Always choose love over the alternative of choosing not to love at all, which is exactly where the enemy wants us! Love is always worth it.

Today, I said no to:

_____

_____

_____

_____

_____

Why did I say no?

_____

_____

_____

_____

_____

Saying no made me feel:

- o Independent
- o Strong
- o Guilty
- o Mean
- o Happy
- o Empowered
- o _____

My no gave me more:

- ○ Time
- ○ Opportunity
- ○ Satisfaction
- ○ Power
- ○ Anxiety

I am now available to say yes to or to do:

_____

_____

_____

_____

_____

Prayer

Not only do I want to say no to love sometimes. I want to close the world out. It seems so evil and sometimes my heart gets crushed in the weight of it. Although I want to run away from it and into Your arms. You just dust me off and help me get the strength to push forward. I cannot change the world like I want but I can change my attitude and figure out more ways to continue to spread love. When I get discouraged, I can look to You for the will to keep going. I will not run; I will fight for love. In Jesus' name. Amen.

Ephesians 6:13 (NIV)

Therefore put on the full armor of God, so that when the day of evil comes, you may be able to stand your ground, and after you have done everything, to stand.

DAY 49

Treat today like a good homemade soup, add all your favorite ingredients, and purposefully, enjoy every spoonful! You can always add more flavor and if it becomes too much, just add water, and try, again.

Today, I said no to:

_____

_____

_____

_____

_____

Why did I say no?

_____

_____

_____

_____

_____

Saying no made me feel:

- o   Independent
- o   Strong
- o   Guilty
- o   Mean
- o   Happy
- o   Empowered
- o   _____

My no gave me more:

- o Time
- o Opportunity
- o Satisfaction
- o Power
- o Anxiety

I am now available to say yes to or to do:

_____

_____

_____

_____

_____

Prayer

You gave all the ingredients for love in Your Word. You said that love is patient, kind, longsuffering. It doesn't keep track of wrongs. Lord, love is You. Let me keep Your ingredients to love in the cabinet of my heart and use it every time I share my life with others. You offered us to taste and know that You are good and Lord, I agree that Your love is delicious, and I can't get enough of it. Thank You for it. In Jesus' name. Amen.

1 Corinthians 13:4-8 (NIV)

Love is patient, love is kind. It does not envy, it does not boast, it is not proud. It does not dishonor others, it is not self-seeking, it is not easily angered, it keeps no record of wrongs. Love does not delight in evil but rejoices with the truth. It always protects, always trusts, always hopes, always perseveres. Love never fails.

DAY 50

The enemy has a habit of presenting us with glistening garbage to try and fool us into believing it's treasure. Yes, beware it's "fool's gold". You are worth more than the finest jewels!

Today, I said no to:

_____

_____

_____

_____

_____

Why did I say no?

_____

_____

_____

_____

_____

Saying no made me feel:

- o   Independent
- o   Strong
- o   Guilty
- o   Mean
- o   Happy
- o   Empowered
- o   _____

My no gave me more:

- ○ Time
- ○ Opportunity
- ○ Satisfaction
- ○ Power
- ○ Anxiety

I am now available to say yes to or to do:

_____

_____

_____

_____

_____

Prayer

You say I am worth it all. You gave Your son, Jesus, as ransom for me. You conquered nations for me. You give me tons of wisdom because You understand her worth to me. She is worth more than rubies and You give her to me freely. I am valuable to You. I don't have to settle for less. I am wonderful, You knit me together in my mother's womb with Your own hands. You thought carefully about my design. You assigned me a purpose and You breathed life into me, and I thank You. In Jesus' name. Amen.

Psalms 139:13-14 (NIV)

For you created my inmost being; you knit me together in my mother's womb. I praise you because I am fearfully and wonderfully made; your works are wonderful; I know that full well.

You've reached the end of Day 50. Take a moment to write your own prayer or tell how God is leading you on your NO Journey:

_____

_____

_____

_____

_____

_____

_____

_____

_____

_____

_____

_____

_____

_____

_____

_____

_____

_____

_____

_____

_____

You're More Than Halfway Through

DAY 51

Weigh the cost of a peace of mind and know that you are worth every bit of it. You must say no for your own sanity and sanctity.

Today, I said no to:

_____

_____

_____

_____

_____

Why did I say no?

_____

_____

_____

_____

_____

Saying no made me feel:

- o Independent
- o Strong
- o Guilty
- o Mean
- o Happy
- o Empowered
- o _____

My no gave me more:

- ○ Time
- ○ Opportunity
- ○ Satisfaction
- ○ Power
- ○ Anxiety

I am now available to say yes to or to do:

_____

_____

_____

_____

_____

Prayer

God please, I know things aren't always what they appear to be. Give me strength when it appears there isn't any. Life when I feel death approaching. Compassion when I want to lash out. Love when I want to hate and feel justified in doing so. Justice when it appears unfair and give me truth to decipher the lies. Give me calm amid my storms. Peace on the edges of chaos and love when I feel surrounded by hate and a hug when I feel the urge to let go. Hold on to me tighter in my moments of weakness and keep me grounded in Your everlasting arms. This walk isn't easy, but the benefits sure outweigh a life without You. In Jesus' name, I praise You. Amen.

Isaiah 26:3 (NIV)

You will keep in perfect peace those whose minds are steadfast because they trust in you.

DAY 52

Stop telling yourself no. You are good enough, strong enough, wise enough, and intelligent enough. Stop getting in the way of God's truth with your lies of self-sabotage. You can do it and you will.

Today, I said no to:

_____

_____

_____

_____

_____

Why did I say no?

_____

_____

_____

_____

_____

Saying no made me feel:

- o Independent
- o Strong
- o Guilty
- o Mean
- o Happy
- o Empowered
- o _____

My no gave me more:

- ○ Time
- ○ Opportunity
- ○ Satisfaction
- ○ Power
- ○ Anxiety

I am now available to say yes to or to do:

_____

_____

_____

_____

_____

Prayer

Thank You for choosing me, equipping me, staying with me, and loving me through it all. Thank You for helping me to stand and keep my head lifted towards the heavens. Thank You for never leaving me or forsaking me. Thank You for blessing my family, friends, and Your children. You are God and God alone and I just thank You for being the Great I Am that You are, in Jesus' name, Amen.

Deuteronomy 31:6 (NIV)

Be strong and courageous. Do not be afraid or terrified because of them, for the LORD your God goes with you; he will never leave you nor forsake you.

DAY 53

Get out of your own way today and accomplish what you have been putting off. If God be for you then who could be against you? No one, not even yourself.

Today, I said no to:

_____
_____
_____
_____
_____

Why did I say no?

_____
_____
_____
_____
_____

Saying no made me feel:

- o   Independent
- o   Strong
- o   Guilty
- o   Mean
- o   Happy
- o   Empowered
- o   _

My no gave me more:

- Time
- Opportunity
- Satisfaction
- Power
- Anxiety

I am now available to say yes to or to do:

_____

_____

_____

_____

_____

Prayer

Let me put self-doubt to the side and suspend its license over my life forever. Help me to close my eyes and ears to negative media and images that I see that cause me to begin comparing myself to others. I need to say no to my own self-sabotage. I need to say no to what the world feels I should look like, sound like, act like and speak like and listen to the One that really matters and that is You, Almighty God. In Jesus' name. Amen.

Matthew 10:30–31 (ESV)

But even the hairs of your head are all numbered. Fear not, therefore; you are of more value than many sparrows.

DAY 54

In your singleness, instead of wondering who he will be, ask God to transform you into the woman He needs you to be so that when he arrives, you'll be ready.

Today, I said no to:

_____

_____

_____

_____

_____

Why did I say no?

_____

_____

_____

_____

_____

Saying no made me feel:

- o   Independent
- o   Strong
- o   Guilty
- o   Mean
- o   Happy
- o   Empowered
- o   _____

My no gave me more:

- ○ Time
- ○ Opportunity
- ○ Satisfaction
- ○ Power
- ○ Anxiety

I am now available to say yes to or to do:

_____

_____

_____

_____

_____

Prayer

Lord, it is easy for me to recite what I desire out of others. It's hard for me to decipher if I am actually meeting the needs of what I want so that when You bring the desires of my heart, I am ready. Lord, make me ready. Prepare a place for me in my future. Let me have realistic expectations for the people in my life and a higher standard for myself, as well. Don't let me get stuck with a one-eyed point of view while reality is blocked from me.

Psalm 37:4 (ESV)

Delight yourself in the Lord, and he will give you the desires of your heart.

DAY 55

Have hope! Do not give up. Do not hang your head in defeat! It is not over. Dust off, stand up and move forward. If there is breath in your body, you MUST keep fighting. There is still purpose in you! There is still reason for you! Keep going.

Today, I said no to:

_____

_____

_____

_____

_____

Why did I say no?

_____

_____

_____

_____

_____

Saying no made me feel:

- o   Independent
- o   Strong
- o   Guilty
- o   Mean
- o   Happy
- o   Empowered
- o   _____

My no gave me more:

- Time
- Opportunity
- Satisfaction
- Power
- Anxiety

I am now available to say yes to or to do:

_____

_____

_____

_____

_____

Prayer

Lord, I AM here for a reason. My reason is to serve You and testify about Your goodness. I don't know what Your plans are for me, but I do know that my life is not in vain. Help me to get in alignment with You. Help me to see me through Your eyes. Help me to zero in on what I have and figure out how to make treasure out of it. You fed the multitude with a little. Surely, what little I think I have; You can have me to do big things with it. So, I am handing it over to You. You know what to do with what You have given to me. I will follow Your lead and finish what You started. In Jesus' name. Amen.

Philippians 1:6 (ESV)

And I am sure of this, that he who began a good work in you will bring it to completion at the day of Jesus Christ.

DAY 56

No matter how foggy it looks, how far it seems or how hopeless "they" say it may be...you keep chipping away, soon it will be yours for the victory!

Today, I said no to:

_____

_____

_____

_____

_____

Why did I say no?

_____

_____

_____

_____

_____

Saying no made me feel:

- ○ Independent
- ○ Strong
- ○ Guilty
- ○ Mean
- ○ Happy
- ○ Empowered
- ○ _____

My no gave me more:

- o Time
- o Opportunity
- o Satisfaction
- o Power
- o Anxiety

I am now available to say yes to or to do:

_____

_____

_____

_____

_____

Prayer

My job is to finish the race You have set before me. I feel like so many obstacles keep getting in the way of the goal. Every time I see the finish line, a detour comes in the road and throws me off track. Lord, thank You for being my Mighty Navigator. You keep finding new paths and giving me keys to unlock doors. You keep telling me I am safe and showing me the right direction to take. You know I am a weary traveler, so You keep sending people that encourage me, provide nourishment, and expertise. I am going to finish because I am not a failure. I will finish because I am complete in You! In Jesus' name. Amen.

Hebrews 12:1 (NIV)

Therefore, since we are surrounded by such a great cloud of witnesses, let us throw off everything that hinders and the sin that so easily entangles, and let us run with perseverance the race marked out for us.

DAY 57

Don't get angry, use foul language, scream, or speak your mind out of frustration; a gentle voice and truthful answer can be just as powerful!

Today, I said no to:

_____

_____

_____

_____

_____

Why did I say no?

_____

_____

_____

_____

_____

Saying no made me feel:

- ○ Independent
- ○ Strong
- ○ Guilty
- ○ Mean
- ○ Happy
- ○ Empowered
- ○ _____

My no gave me more:

- o Time
- o Opportunity
- o Satisfaction
- o Power
- o Anxiety

I am now available to say yes to or to do:

_____

_____

_____

_____

_____

Prayer

Lord, let my approach be calming, my touch be gentle and mighty and my words...let my words be like honey...sweet going in, smooth going down and healing all the way. Let my ears be a funnel to my heart, filtering out all nonsense and taking in only what is good for me. Don't let me get distracted by the noise but hear Your silent, peaceful voice within it because I know it's in there somewhere. Just give me the discernment to hear it. In Jesus' name. Amen.

Proverbs 15:1-3 (ESV)

A gentle answer turns away wrath, but a harsh word stirs up anger. The tongue of the wise commends knowledge, but the mouth of the fool gushes folly. The eyes of the LORD are everywhere, keeping watch on the wicked and the good.

DAY 58

The brightest star in the sky sits outside your window. Jesus, the brightest light not of this world, lives inside you. Never forget who and whose you are and keep shining brightly. You may be the only light some will ever see.

Today, I said no to:

_____

_____

_____

_____

_____

Why did I say no?

_____

_____

_____

_____

_____

Saying no made me feel:

- o Independent
- o Strong
- o Guilty
- o Mean
- o Happy
- o Empowered
- o _____

My no gave me more:

- ○ Time
- ○ Opportunity
- ○ Satisfaction
- ○ Power
- ○ Anxiety

I am now available to say yes to or to do:

_____

_____

_____

_____

_____

Prayer

Let me shine! Let me shine! Lord, on my darkest days let me shine. Let me add light to every situation. Let my energy be positive and change atmospheres. When I go to work, class, home, and to visit others let me shine because when people see me glowing, they will know that it is not me that is vibrantly shining it is the Lord within me. Entire environments will shift out of respect for the Lord. Let my behavior be so impressionable and my spirit be so positively intoxicating that others will want to know my God! In Jesus' name. Amen.

John 14:6 (NIV)

Jesus answered, "I am the way and the truth and the life. No one comes to the Father except through me."

DAY 59

Don't be so focused on one thing that you lose sight of everything else. Distractions can make you say "yes" out of guilt instead of "no" out of wisdom.

Today, I said no to:

_____

_____

_____

_____

_____

Why did I say no?

_____

_____

_____

_____

_____

Saying no made me feel:

- o Independent
- o Strong
- o Guilty
- o Mean
- o Happy
- o Empowered
- o _____

My no gave me more:

- ○ Time
- ○ Opportunity
- ○ Satisfaction
- ○ Power
- ○ Anxiety

I am now available to say yes to or to do:

_____

_____

_____

_____

_____

Prayer

I only want to be consumed with You. Help me know how to divide my time wisely. I do so much in a day, I hardly find time for me. The guilt of my busyness even makes me say yes to things that I really shouldn't. Help me put things in perspective. I work hard for my loved ones to have nice things, but You will provide. I am asking You to help me carve out quality time for my family and my personal care. I know we are not promised tomorrow and I get so afraid that I will miss out because of my schedule. Lord, give me wisdom with my time and don't let fear rule my decisions. In Jesus' name. Amen.

Psalms 1:1-6 (NIV)

Blessed is the one who does not walk in step with the wicked or stand in the way that sinners take or sit in the company of mockers, but whose delight is in the law of the LORD, and who meditates on his law day and night.

DAY 60

Real power is having the ability to get what you want but exercising the strength to refrain or say no.

Today, I said no to:

_____

_____

_____

_____

_____

Why did I say no?

_____

_____

_____

_____

_____

Saying no made me feel:

- o Independent
- o Strong
- o Guilty
- o Mean
- o Happy
- o Empowered
- o _____

My no gave me more:

- ○ Time
- ○ Opportunity
- ○ Satisfaction
- ○ Power
- ○ Anxiety

I am now available to say yes to or to do:

_____

_____

_____

_____

_____

Prayer

It feels so good to have options and even better to have the ability to choose. Lord, You gave us the ability to choose. Help me to make wise decisions with my choices and not be greedy. Help me to exercise restraint and not overdue or underachieve. Although I can say yes to so many things, help me discern which really need my help and attention and which ones will be better for someone else to manage. I do not have to have it all. I have You and You are plenty, Lord. In Jesus' name. Amen.

Job 22:21 (NIV)

Submit to God and be at peace with him; in this way prosperity will come to you.

You've reached the end of Day 60. Take a moment to write your own prayer or tell how God is leading you on your NO Journey:

_____

_____

_____

_____

_____

_____

_____

_____

_____

_____

_____

_____

_____

_____

_____

_____

_____

_____

_____

_____

_____

The Best is Yet to Come

DAY 61

Not living out your potential can be haunting and rob you of your dreams. Only when you begin doing what you are purposed to do will you get a full night's sleep.

Today, I said no to:

_____

_____

_____

_____

_____

Why did I say no?

_____

_____

_____

_____

_____

Saying no made me feel:

- o Independent
- o Strong
- o Guilty
- o Mean
- o Happy
- o Empowered
- o _____

My no gave me more:

- o Time
- o Opportunity
- o Satisfaction
- o Power
- o Anxiety

I am now available to say yes to or to do:

_____

_____

_____

_____

_____

Prayer

Don't let Satan get the best of me. Don't let him kill my potential. Help me to stop procrastinating and move on. Time stands still for no one, and it feels like the clock is speeding up. I have dreams. I have goals I want to achieve outside of my career and my family. Please close the door on fear when it comes creeping in. It paralyzes me. I begin to feel lost. Somehow, when I put my mind on You, my energy comes back. I start but I have trouble finishing. Lord, give me that boost to get things done. Help me recognize the enemy and his many distractions. Let me stay focused and ready to do the marvelous works You have placed in me! It's not too late. In Jesus' name. Amen.

John 10:10 (NIV)

The thief comes only to steal and kill and destroy; I have come that they may have life and have it to the full.

DAY 62

Don't waste your time trying to teach a fool. It's like adding purified water to a bucket with a hole in it...a waste.

Today, I said no to:

_____

_____

_____

_____

_____

Why did I say no?

_____

_____

_____

_____

Saying no made me feel:

- Independent
- Strong
- Guilty
- Mean
- Happy
- Empowered
- _____

My no gave me more:

- o Time
- o Opportunity
- o Satisfaction
- o Power
- o Anxiety

I am now available to say yes to or to do:

_____

_____

_____

_____

_____

Prayer

Please help me to stop wasting my time on foolishness with people who aren't even trying to understand or be better. Surround me with people who want to grow and learn. Put me in a place where I can teach and be taught. Hold my tongue when I want to argue with or talk sense into someone incapable of listening to what I have to say. Help me to spot the drama and avoid it because I don't have to indulge. In Jesus' name. Amen.

Proverbs 9:7-9 (NIV)

Whoever corrects a mocker invites insult; whoever rebukes the wicked incurs abuse. Do not rebuke mockers or they will hate you; rebuke the wise man and they will love you. Instruct the wise and they will be wiser still; teach the righteous and they will add to their learning.

DAY 63

Don't get discouraged when things don't go as you planned. God is still working out the kinks for your benefit.

Today, I said no to:

_____

_____

_____

_____

_____

Why did I say no?

_____

_____

_____

_____

_____

Saying no made me feel:

- o   Independent
- o   Strong
- o   Guilty
- o   Mean
- o   Happy
- o   Empowered
- o   _____

My no gave me more:

- o Time
- o Opportunity
- o Satisfaction
- o Power
- o Anxiety

I am now available to say yes to or to do:

_____

_____

_____

_____

_____

Prayer

I am learning to be patient and wait on You, Lord. I always seem to run into problems when I decide to do things ahead of Your schedule. I want to trust You more. I want to increase my faith in You. Bless me with an abundance of both. I see my pride bleeding through when I try to take control of a situation that You already have handled. Lord, I repent. You are my Helper in times of trouble and when I am in need. I must wait on You. I will wait on You because You have me in Your heart, and You want what is best for my life. Scribble that in my mind so I never forget. In Jesus' name. Amen.

Isaiah 40:31 (KJV)

But they that wait upon the Lord shall renew their strength; they shall mount up with wings as eagles; they shall run, and not be weary; and they shall walk, and not faint...

DAY 64

Even when we can't see our way clearly, we must trust God.

Today, I said no to:

_____

_____

_____

_____

_____

Why did I say no?

_____

_____

_____

_____

_____

Saying no made me feel:

- o Independent
- o Strong
- o Guilty
- o Mean
- o Happy
- o Empowered
- o _____

My no gave me more:

- Time
- Opportunity
- Satisfaction
- Power
- Anxiety

I am now available to say yes to or to do:

_____

_____

_____

_____

_____

Prayer

Sometimes I have a hard time trying to figure everything out and it all seems to get stuck together. Help me to sort things out and get my life in order. Help me put things in proper perspective. Help me to clip away dead ends. Help me to smooth out bumpy situations and see my way through the fog so Your light can shine through. In Jesus' name. Amen.

Ecclesiastes 3:1-5 (ESV)

For everything there is a season, and a time for every matter under heaven: a time to be born, and a time to die; a time to plant, and a time to pluck up what is planted; a time to kill, and a time to heal; a time to break down, and a time to build up; a time to weep, and a time to laugh; a time to mourn, and a time to dance; a time to cast away stones, and a time to gather stones together; a time to embrace, and a time to refrain from embracing...

DAY 65

You better PUSH! Push past the naysayers, push past the limitations and handicaps, and push past your own doubt and fears. And PULL! Pull up a chair in the driver's seat to your life and take control of every thought and word that comes out of your mouth. Fill your I can't and I won't with I will and I can because He will and He can!

Today, I said no to:

_____
_____
_____
_____
_____

Why did I say no?

_____
_____
_____
_____
_____

Saying no made me feel:

- o Independent
- o Strong
- o Guilty
- o Mean
- o Happy
- o Empowered
- o _____

My no gave me more:

- o Time
- o Opportunity
- o Satisfaction
- o Power
- o Anxiety

I am now available to say yes to or to do:

_____

_____

_____

_____

_____

Prayer

I can do this. I can accomplish what I set out to do. God, You are with me. Help me to search You out and see You in every room I enter. I am in control because You are in control. I speak life because You are my life. Take captive everything vile that comes out of me and destroy it. Continue to pour goodness and love into me. Help me to recognize the fruits the Holy Spirit has placed inside of me and let me plant seeds of success all around. In Jesus' name. Amen.

2 Corinthians 10:5 (NIV)

We demolish arguments and every pretension that sets itself up against the knowledge of God, and we take captive every thought to make it obedient to Christ.

DAY 66

Think about tomorrow as you live in today; not in fear of the future but in hope for a better one!

Today, I said no to:

_____

_____

_____

_____

_____

Why did I say no?

_____

_____

_____

_____

Saying no made me feel:

- o Independent
- o Strong
- o Guilty
- o Mean
- o Happy
- o Empowered
- o _____

My no gave me more:

- Time
- Opportunity
- Satisfaction
- Power
- Anxiety

I am now available to say yes to or to do:

_____

_____

_____

_____

_____

Prayer

I am excited about the future, although I know it is promised to no one. I do know the future brings second chances and first times, whether it's tomorrow or the next moment. It brings hope and opportunity. Change in me what needs to be changed today so I can look forward to reaping the results. It is a brand-new day, and I am brand new, too. I am constantly changing and trusting the changes are for my good. In Jesus' name. Amen.

Lamentations 3:23 (NIV)

They are new every morning; great is your faithfulness.

DAY 67

To solve a problem, you must become an active part of the solution!

Today, I said no to:

_____

_____

_____

_____

_____

Why did I say no?

_____

_____

_____

_____

_____

Saying no made me feel:

- o Independent
- o Strong
- o Guilty
- o Mean
- o Happy
- o Empowered
- o _____

My no gave me more:

- ○ Time
- ○ Opportunity
- ○ Satisfaction
- ○ Power
- ○ Anxiety

I am now available to say yes to or to do:

_____

_____

_____

_____

_____

Prayer

Lord, I don't want to just be a talker. I also don't want to be like a general spouting out orders without putting in any work myself. Let me also be a part of the solution, so my team can know I care just as much as they do. Let me set a good example. Help me to build a good reputation and respect amongst my colleagues. I want to be a team player not a one-man band. I want us to work together. Help me to encourage them. Help me to empower them to be their best. Be with me and in me at my workplace so Your light can shine through me, and my intentions stay pure and trusted. In Jesus' name. Amen.

1 Corinthians 12:14 (KJV)

For the body is not one member, but many.

DAY 68

If enough people are calling you a horse, it might be time for you to saddle up. What they say may not be true but it's worth investigating the accusation!

Today, I said no to:

_____

_____

_____

_____

_____

Why did I say no?

_____

_____

_____

_____

_____

Saying no made me feel:

- o Independent
- o Strong
- o Guilty
- o Mean
- o Happy
- o Empowered
- o _____

My no gave me more:

- ○ Time
- ○ Opportunity
- ○ Satisfaction
- ○ Power
- ○ Anxiety

I am now available to say yes to or to do:

_____

_____

_____

_____

_____

Prayer

It is hard for me to see myself from the perspective of others, especially when they are saying something about me that I find to be negative. Help me to go beyond my feelings and really hear what others are saying to me or about me. Create in me a clean heart. Please don't let pride prevent me from prevailing. Let me truly look at myself. Lord, I will put it on the table, and I want You to give me the truth. If You say it is so, help me make the adjustments I need to change. When You make the changes in me, I know others will see it and I know it will be for the good of us all. I know Jesus cannot abide in a lie, so let the truth show through me. In Jesus' name. Amen.

2 Corinthians 13:5 (NIV)

Examine yourselves to see whether you are in the faith; test yourselves. Do you not realize that Christ Jesus is in you—unless, of course, you fail the test?

DAY 69

Get out of your own way, can't you see brilliance is trying to enter?

Today, I said no to:

_____

_____

_____

_____

_____

Why did I say no?

_____

_____

_____

_____

Saying no made me feel:

- ○ Independent
- ○ Strong
- ○ Guilty
- ○ Mean
- ○ Happy
- ○ Empowered
- ○ _____

My no gave me more:

- ○ Time
- ○ Opportunity
- ○ Satisfaction
- ○ Power
- ○ Anxiety

I am now available to say yes to or to do:

_____

_____

_____

_____

_____

Prayer

Lord, could I really be guilty of self-sabotage. Am I procrastinating. I pray against it! Lord, I rebuke fear, worry, doubt. You are my strength. You are my champion. The Holy Spirit is my guide. I am not afraid. I can do all that You have purposed me to do. I am blessed in my skills. I am Your child and there is no reason for me not to be good at what I do. Help me to learn as much as I can in my field, so I am confident. Give me the tools and resources I need so I am prepared. Lord, send people who will speak words of encouragement and wisdom when they see me retreating to my comfort zone. I cannot doubt myself any longer if I claim to believe You have gifted me and I won't. In Jesus' name. Amen.

Romans 10:11 (NIV)

Anyone who believes in Him will never be put to shame.

DAY 70

Make sure your mouth is as quick to apologize as your temper is to flare up.

Today, I said no to:

_____
_____
_____
_____
_____

Why did I say no?

_____
_____
_____
_____
_____

Saying no made me feel:

- o   Independent
- o   Strong
- o   Guilty
- o   Mean
- o   Happy
- o   Empowered
- o   _____

My no gave me more:

- ○ Time
- ○ Opportunity
- ○ Satisfaction
- ○ Power
- ○ Anxiety

I am now available to say yes to or to do:

_____

_____

_____

_____

_____

Prayer

Pride is a fool's game, Lord, don't let me play it. When I am wrong, please prick my soul. Open my mouth and make sincere words of apology come out. Don't let me feel guilty or ashamed afterwards for doing the right thing. Help me bare whatever comes after with humility and a lighthearted spirit. Let me laugh at myself when I make mistakes and be the first to apologize. In Jesus' name. Amen.

James 5:16 (NLT)

Confess your sins to each other and pray for each other so that you may be healed. The earnest prayer of a righteous person has great power and produces wonderful results.

You've reached the end of Day 70. Take a moment to write your own prayer or tell how God is leading you on your NO Journey:

_____

_____

_____

_____

_____

_____

_____

_____

_____

_____

_____

_____

_____

_____

_____

_____

_____

_____

_____

_____

_____

_____

Time for the Homestretch

THE NEXT PHASE OF MY NO JOURNEY IS ALL ABOUT MAKING DECLARATIONS, AFFIRMATIONS, AND RECOMMENDATIONS TO MYSELF

IT'S TIME TO BE HONEST ABOUT HOW YOU MAY BE FEELING AND DO SOME SELF-CARE. DON'T JUST SAY THESE WORDS IN YOUR MIND, SPEAK THEM OUT LOUD. YOU ARE DOING GREAT. JUST KEEP GOING!

DAY 71

Today I will say no to crying and talking myself out of expressing my true feelings instead of speaking up!

Today, I said no to:

_____

_____

_____

_____

_____

Why did I say no?

_____

_____

_____

_____

Saying no made me feel:

- o Independent
- o Strong
- o Guilty
- o Mean
- o Happy
- o Empowered
- o _____

My no gave me more:

- o Time
- o Opportunity
- o Satisfaction
- o Power
- o Anxiety

I am now available to say yes to or to do:

_____

_____

_____

_____

_____

Prayer

I said no for a reason. Turn my tears into diamonds and let them be valuable to my spirit. I am worthy of good things. I should stand up for myself because I don't deserve to be bullied emotionally, physically, or spiritually. And Holy Spirit, when I can't find the words, speak on my behalf. Don't let my words make it worse but make it for my good. In Jesus' name. Amen.

- ✓ I don't deserve to be talked down to.
- ✓ I do deserve to be heard and treated with respect.
- ✓ I will speak up for myself and others treated unjustly.

Romans 8:26 (NIV)

We do not know what we ought to pray for, but the Spirit himself intercedes for us through wordless groans.

DAY 72

Today I will say no to denying myself good things while others selfishly indulge.

Today, I said no to:

_____

_____

_____

_____

_____

Why did I say no?

_____

_____

_____

_____

Saying no made me feel:

- o Independent
- o Strong
- o Guilty
- o Mean
- o Happy
- o Empowered
- o _____

My no gave me more:

- o Time
- o Opportunity
- o Satisfaction
- o Power
- o Anxiety

I am now available to say yes to or to do:

_____

_____

_____

_____

_____

Prayer

Lord, I do not mind being the last person to receive, even if I don't get anything at all because I know You got me. However, there are times when I let people go before me who did not put in the work or the effort. Take away the feelings of guilt that I have for denying myself because it leads to regret, especially when I feel justified. I am worthy and it is okay for me to partake. Help me to see that. Reward me in front of my enemies and I'll give You the glory, Almighty God. In Jesus' name. Amen.

- ✓ I don't always have to eat last.
- ✓ God delights in me.
- ✓ I deserve a seat at the table.

Psalms 23:5 (NIV)

You prepare a table before me in the presence of my enemies; you anoint my head with oil; my cup overflows.

DAY 73

Today I will say no to feeling like I don't deserve better when I really do. (Jesus, died for me. So, I am every bit of worth it!)

Today, I said no to:

_____

_____

_____

_____

_____

Why did I say no?

_____

_____

_____

_____

_____

Saying no made me feel:

- ○ Independent
- ○ Strong
- ○ Guilty
- ○ Mean
- ○ Happy
- ○ Empowered
- ○ _____

My no gave me more:

- Time
- Opportunity
- Satisfaction
- Power
- Anxiety

I am now available to say yes to or to do:

_____

_____

_____

_____

_____

Prayer

You sealed me with Your stamp of approval. I deserve to be here. I deserve good things. I have been forgiven, redeemed, and replenished. You are my God. You are my Father. Everything is Yours to give and You give me plenty. You gave Your life for me to have life. In Jesus' name. Amen.

- ✓ I deserve good things.
- ✓ I am good and forgiven.
- ✓ I am priceless!

1 Peter 1:18–19 (NIV)

For you know that it was not perishable things such as silver or gold that you were redeemed from the empty way of life handed down to you from your ancestors, but with the precious blood of Christ, a lamb without blemish or defect.

DAY 74

Today I will say no to acting like I can take it when really, I can't take it.

Today, I said no to:

_____

_____

_____

_____

_____

Why did I say no?

_____

_____

_____

_____

_____

Saying no made me feel:

- o   Independent
- o   Strong
- o   Guilty
- o   Mean
- o   Happy
- o   Empowered
- o   _____

My no gave me more:

- o   Time
- o   Opportunity
- o   Satisfaction
- o   Power
- o   Anxiety

I am now available to say yes to or to do:

_____

_____

_____

_____

_____

Prayer

It's okay for me to admit when I am hurting. It is okay for me to say when I am filled to capacity and cannot take anymore. Help me to stop hiding my feelings and acting like things don't affect me because they do. Soothe my brokenness and fill me with Your love. In Jesus' name. Amen.

- ✓   It's okay to express my true feelings.
- ✓   I don't always need to be strong.
- ✓   I don't have to prove anything to anyone but God.
- ✓   My tears cleanse my soul.
- ✓   Crying does help me feel better.

Psalms 147:3 (NIV)

He heals the brokenhearted and binds up their wounds.

DAY 75

Today I will say no to feeling guilty about standing up for myself. Even if I am wrong, at least I did it! I will apologize or admit my mistake but pat myself on the back for taking my power back.

Today, I said no to:

_____

_____

_____

_____

_____

Why did I say no?

_____

_____

_____

_____

_____

Saying no made me feel:

- o Independent
- o Strong
- o Guilty
- o Mean
- o Happy
- o Empowered
- o _____

My no gave me more:

- o   Time
- o   Opportunity
- o   Satisfaction
- o   Power
- o   Anxiety

I am now available to say yes to or to do:

_____

_____

_____

_____

_____

Prayer

I have been quiet for far too long, Lord. I wasn't silent because I was letting You fight all my battles. I was silent because I was afraid to speak up. I was silent because I didn't want to cause any problems. Forgive me for being a peacekeeper instead of a peacemaker. I should have stood up sooner but thank You for the courage to stand up now! In Jesus' name. Amen.

- ✓   I have a voice and an opinion.
- ✓   I can fight my battles and not be afraid.
- ✓   A peacekeeper hides the truth, a peacemaker reveals it. I will reveal truths. I am a Peacemaker!

Matthew 5:9 (NIV)

Blessed are the peacemakers, for they will be called children of God.

DAY 76

Today I will say no to letting people invade my personal space without permission.

Today, I said no to:

_____

_____

_____

_____

_____

Why did I say no?

_____

_____

_____

_____

Saying no made me feel:

- o Independent
- o Strong
- o Guilty
- o Mean
- o Happy
- o Empowered
- o _____

My no gave me more:

- Time
- Opportunity
- Satisfaction
- Power
- Anxiety

I am now available to say yes to or to do:

_____

_____

_____

_____

_____

Prayer

I have a right to privacy. I have a right to my own personal space and peace of mind. You made my body my own, accept to my spouse. No one has a right to invade my space without my permission. Help me stand up to those who want to dump their garbage on me or in my space. Give me the willpower to tell them no. I want to fill my space with good things like joy, faith, happiness, good deeds, and positivity. In Jesus' name. Amen.

- ✓ I have a right to keeping my mind, body, soul and property clean, healthy, and positive.
- ✓ I don't have to let negativity into my personal space.

Acts 17:26 (ESV)

And he made from one man every nation of mankind to live on all the face of the earth, having determined allotted periods and the boundaries of their dwelling place...

DAY 77

Today I will say no to meaningless conversations with meaningless people! (I have better things to do than take in someone else's drama. They go on and I am left feeling blah!)

Today, I said no to:

_____

_____

_____

_____

_____

Why did I say no?

_____

_____

_____

_____

_____

Saying no made me feel:

- o   Independent
- o   Strong
- o   Guilty
- o   Mean
- o   Happy
- o   Empowered
- o   _____

My no gave me more:

- o Time
- o Opportunity
- o Satisfaction
- o Power
- o Anxiety

I am now available to say yes to or to do:

_____

_____

_____

_____

_____

Prayer

If people are coming to me with negative conversations or gossip, I don't have to listen. Help me to turn them away softly. If conversations do not edify You or speak of doing good, block them from my ears. Give me a spirit of discernment so I can know when to walk away from negative talk that stirs up trouble. Let me know the difference between advocating for justice and participating in negativity, so I can choose wisely. In Jesus' name. Amen.

- ✓ I will attract positive people doing positive things.
- ✓ Gossipers will beware of my path.
- ✓ I will speak and repeat things that edify and exalt others.

Psalms 34:1-3 (NIV)

I will extol the LORD at all times; his praise will always be on my lips. I will glory in the LORD; let the afflicted hear and rejoice. Glorify the LORD with me; let us exalt his name together.

DAY 78

Today I am saying no to people who make me feel small or even guilty to cover up their own insecurities.

Today, I said no to:

_____

_____

_____

_____

_____

Why did I say no?

_____

_____

_____

_____

_____

Saying no made me feel:

- ○ Independent
- ○ Strong
- ○ Guilty
- ○ Mean
- ○ Happy
- ○ Empowered
- ○ _____

My no gave me more:

- o Time
- o Opportunity
- o Satisfaction
- o Power
- o Anxiety

I am now available to say yes to or to do:

_____

_____

_____

_____

_____

Prayer

Lord, please protect me from the abuse of others. Do not let people speak ill of me behind my back or in my face. Do not let them abuse me emotionally, physically, or verbally. I do not have to feel guilty about wrong things being done to me because someone is not having a good day or going through a rough time in their life. I am nobody's dumping ground. Protect me from people like that. In Jesus' name. Amen.

- ✓ I deserve respect.
- ✓ My body is a temple of the Lord and shouldn't be abused.
- ✓ I am a child of God and protected by His blood.

John 13:34 (ESV)

A new commandment I give to you, that you love one another: just as I have loved you, you also are to love one another.

DAY 79

Today I am saying no to children who think they know more than I do but haven't been on this earth nearly as long or experienced half of what I have because I made sure they didn't have to.

Today, I said no to:

_____
_____
_____
_____
_____

Why did I say no?

_____
_____
_____
_____
_____

Saying no made me feel:

- o Independent
- o Strong
- o Guilty
- o Mean
- o Happy
- o Empowered
- o _____

My no gave me more:

- o Time
- o Opportunity
- o Satisfaction
- o Power
- o Anxiety

I am now available to say yes to or to do:

_____

_____

_____

_____

_____

Prayer

Lord, help my children to understand what it means to respect and honor their parents. Let them take heed to wisdom. I am tired of telling them the same things, repeatedly and them brushing off my words. Lord, let them see my advice as relevant. Let them see that I am trying to help them be better and avoid some pitfalls. Lord, I lay them at Your feet. In Jesus' name. Amen.

- ✓ I will speak to those who listen.
- ✓ I am okay with loving my children from a distance.
- ✓ I am okay with letting go and letting God.

Ephesians 6:1-3 (ESV)

Children, obey your parents in the Lord, for this is right. "Honor your father and mother" (this is the first commandment with a promise), "that it may go well with you and that you may live long in the land."

DAY 80

Today I am saying no to people who feel like I owe them something because they did something nice for me. (Was it really to make me feel good or to make you feel better?)

Today, I said no to:

_____

_____

_____

_____

_____

Why did I say no?

_____

_____

_____

_____

_____

Saying no made me feel:

- o Independent
- o Strong
- o Guilty
- o Mean
- o Happy
- o Empowered
- o _____

My no gave me more:

- Time
- Opportunity
- Satisfaction
- Power
- Anxiety

I am now available to say yes to or to do:

_____

_____

_____

_____

_____

Prayer

Bless the hearts of those who help me. Let my helpers do it out of kindness. Bless them with an overflow, Almighty God. Let me see those who are sincerely trying to help and avoid those who help so they can boast or for personal gain. I do not want pride to block my blessings, but I pray wisdom oversees them. Thank You because all good things come from You. In Jesus' name. Amen.

Matthew 6:2-4 (NIV)

Thus, when you give to the needy, sound no trumpet before you, as the hypocrites do in the synagogues and in the streets, that they may be praised by others. Truly, I say to you, they have received their reward. But when you give to the needy, do not let your left hand know what your right hand is doing, so that your giving may be in secret. And your Father who sees in secret will reward you.

You've reached the end of Day 80. Take a moment to write your own prayer or tell how God is leading you on your NO Journey:

_____

_____

_____

_____

_____

_____

_____

_____

_____

_____

_____

_____

_____

_____

_____

_____

_____

_____

_____

_____

_____

_____

Almost to the Finish Line

DAY 81

Today I say no to gifts and favors with strings attached. (Keep them, I'm good and I probably don't need them anyway!)

Today, I said no to:

_____

_____

_____

_____

_____

Why did I say no?

_____

_____

_____

_____

Saying no made me feel:

- o Independent
- o Strong
- o Guilty
- o Mean
- o Happy
- o Empowered
- o _____

My no gave me more:

- Time
- Opportunity
- Satisfaction
- Power
- Anxiety

I am now available to say yes to or to do:

_____

_____

_____

_____

_____

Prayer

Place in me a clean heart, Lord. Let me give to people without expectation. If I loan money, let me not expect them to return it so I can rejoice when they do. Let me give because I have it to give. Let people give to me because they can, and they want to. Better yet, Lord, let what I have be enough. Put me in a position where all my accounts say, "paid in full". Your grace is sufficient for me. In Jesus' name. Amen.

- ✓ I have an excess and abundance.
- ✓ I pay debts and am in good standing.
- ✓ I give in love and am blessed to receive in love.

Luke 6:35-36 (NIV)

But love your enemies, do good, and lend, expecting nothing in return. Your reward will be great, and you will be children of the Most High; for he is kind to the ungrateful and the wicked. Be merciful, just as your Father is merciful...

DAY 82

Today I am saying no to people who rob my energy but don't replace it with anything good, so I am drained once again!

Today, I said no to:

_____

_____

_____

_____

_____

Why did I say no?

_____

_____

_____

_____

Saying no made me feel:

- o Independent
- o Strong
- o Guilty
- o Mean
- o Happy
- o Empowered
- o _____

My no gave me more:

- Time
- Opportunity
- Satisfaction
- Power
- Anxiety

I am now available to say yes to or to do:

_____

_____

_____

_____

_____

Prayer

Protect me from Takers. Those who take and have nothing positive to give. People who just come around like scavengers and bottom feeders. Those who are ungrateful and never satisfied with what they have. People who want to take until I am empty, and they are full. Protect my heart from the heartbreakers. Draw me near those that will benefit from my help and help others in return. Pour into me, Lord, so I can have capacity to pour into others. In Jesus' name. Amen.

- ✓ All that I have belongs to the Lord, no one can take from me but to Him, they must give an account.
- ✓ My riches are stored in heaven.
- ✓ I am blessed to give my energy to those in need.

Proverbs 11:24 (ESV)

One gives freely, yet grows all the richer; another withholds what he should give, and only suffers want.

DAY 83

Today I am saying no to church folks and everyday folks who see me struggling but won't ask if I need help but will ask me to join their ministry or participate in their event. (Lord, help us all!)

Today, I said no to:

_____

_____

_____

_____

_____

Why did I say no?

_____

_____

_____

_____

_____

Saying no made me feel:

- o Independent
- o Strong
- o Guilty
- o Mean
- o Happy
- o Empowered
- o _____

My no gave me more:

- ○ Time
- ○ Opportunity
- ○ Satisfaction
- ○ Power
- ○ Anxiety

I am now available to say yes to or to do:

_____

_____

_____

_____

_____

Prayer

Holy Spirit, check me before I check others. Help me to see people and be concerned with how they are doing. Let me be conscious of the people who surround me. Also, let us care about each other, no matter the color, gender, ability, politics, or rank. Let us be considerate of each other's feelings and get to know one another personally. In Jesus' name. Amen.

- ✓ My time and space are valuable, I will use it wisely.
- ✓ I am considerate of others and myself.
- ✓ I am available for those who need me.
- ✓ I can help out when I have free time to spare.
- ✓ I will be honest about my time and commitments.
- ✓ My first ministry is to my home.

1 Corinthians 10:24 (ESV)

Let no one seek his own good, but the good of his neighbor.

DAY 84

Today I am saying no to people who say they love me, but their actions prove otherwise. (Peace out!)

Today, I said no to:

_____

_____

_____

_____

_____

Why did I say no?

_____

_____

_____

_____

Saying no made me feel:

- ○ Independent
- ○ Strong
- ○ Guilty
- ○ Mean
- ○ Happy
- ○ Empowered
- ○ _____

My no gave me more:

- Time
- Opportunity
- Satisfaction
- Power
- Anxiety

I am now available to say yes to or to do:

_____

_____

_____

_____

_____

Prayer

Actions speak so much louder than the words of people who claim to have my best interest at heart but seem to do otherwise. Help me to take these types of people out of my life. Let me recognize them from a mile away so that I can go in the other direction. Help me to open my mouth and nicely tell them that I am not interested in what they have to say. Don't let me feel like I am obligated to respond to their empty requests. Help me reclaim my no. In Jesus' name. Amen.

- ✓ I am worthy of true love.
- ✓ I will attract friends who don't mean me any harm.
- ✓ I will listen to the Holy Spirit when He tells me to beware.

Colossians 2:8 (NIV)

See to it that no one takes you captive through hollow and deceptive philosophy, which depends on human tradition and the elemental spiritual forces of this world rather than on Christ.

DAY 85

Today I am saying no to people who drain me of money and resources but never give back or try to help when I am in need!

Today, I said no to:

_____

_____

_____

_____

_____

Why did I say no?

_____

_____

_____

_____

Saying no made me feel:

- o   Independent
- o   Strong
- o   Guilty
- o   Mean
- o   Happy
- o   Empowered
- o   _____

My no gave me more:

- o Time
- o Opportunity
- o Satisfaction
- o Power
- o Anxiety

I am now available to say yes to or to do:

_____

_____

_____

_____

_____

Prayer

Lord, don't let me fall for the schemes of the enemy. You give to me in abundance so that I can bless others and tell them about Your goodness. Protect me from those who want to claim what they have not earned and take what isn't theirs to give. They are like the enemy who comes to steal, kill, and destroy. Let the users in my life reveal themselves. Don't let them continue to burden me. In Jesus' name. Amen.

- ✓ I don't owe anyone anything except God.
- ✓ Guilt and fear are not welcome into my life.
- ✓ I will not be taken advantage of anymore.

Proverbs 20:17 (NKJV)

Bread gained by deceit is sweet to a man, but afterward his mouth will be full of gravel.

DAY 86

Today I am saying no to people who lie, cheat, and steal but resent me for doing the right thing!

Today, I said no to:

_____
_____
_____
_____
_____

Why did I say no?

_____
_____
_____
_____
_____

Saying no made me feel:

- o Independent
- o Strong
- o Guilty
- o Mean
- o Happy
- o Empowered
- o _____

My no gave me more:

- ○ Time
- ○ Opportunity
- ○ Satisfaction
- ○ Power
- ○ Anxiety

I am now available to say yes to or to do:

_____

_____

_____

_____

_____

Prayer

Lord, protect me from the haters. I try to stay in my place and mind my own business, but they always find a way to creep back into my life. Lord, keep my name out of their mouths and off their minds. Fill their destructive minds with goodness so when they think about cursing me, blessings come out instead. In Jesus' name. Amen.

- ✓ I will establish healthy relationships and boundaries.
- ✓ I am a good friend who can have good friends.
- ✓ I am protected against toxic people with toxic ideas.

Proverbs 6:16–19 (NIV)

There are six things the LORD hates, seven that are detestable to him: haughty eyes, a lying tongue, hands that shed innocent blood, a heart that devises wicked schemes, feet that are quick to rush into evil, a false witness who pours out lies and a person who stirs up conflict in the community.

DAY 87

Today I am saying no to children that love for me to keep, take care of, and feed their children but never give any money, food, or appreciation for my time because they assume this is not only what I enjoy doing, but what I am supposed to do. (Yeah, right!)

Today, I said no to:

_____
_____
_____
_____
_____

Why did I say no?

_____
_____
_____
_____
_____

Saying no made me feel:

- o   Independent
- o   Strong
- o   Guilty
- o   Mean
- o   Happy
- o   Empowered
- o   _____

My no gave me more:

- ○ Time
- ○ Opportunity
- ○ Satisfaction
- ○ Power
- ○ Anxiety

I am now available to say yes to or to do:

_____

_____

_____

_____

_____

Prayer

Lord, thank You for giving me the courage to stand up for myself. I understand that I must even protect myself from my own children. I do not feel like they purposely are trying to harm me but when they are not considerate of my feelings, time, or money spent it hurts. Help me to deal with them in love and them to respect and honor my feelings and space. I love all of my family, but I need them to understand all I am asking for is respect and consideration. I do not need them to decide for me. I am fully capable of appropriating my own time, food, and finances. Help them to see, I have raised my own children so anything else I do is extra and out of kindness not obligation. In Jesus' name. Amen.

Matthew 19:5 (NIV)

And said, 'For this reason a man will leave his father and mother and be united to his wife, and the two will become one flesh'?

DAY 88

Today I am saying no to jobs that want every bit of my strength, time, intelligence, and ideas but pay me and or treat me less than I deserve. (Work is a two-way negotiation; I do my job and do it well, my job pays me and treats me well. We both should be satisfied.)

Today, I said no to:

_____

_____

_____

_____

_____

Why did I say no?

_____

_____

_____

_____

_____

Saying no made me feel:

- o   Independent
- o   Strong
- o   Guilty
- o   Mean
- o   Happy
- o   Empowered
- o   _____

My no gave me more:

- ○ Time
- ○ Opportunity
- ○ Satisfaction
- ○ Power
- ○ Anxiety

I am now available to say yes to or to do:

_____

_____

_____

_____

_____

Prayer

I pray I am a good worker. I pray I bring sunshine into my work atmosphere and not clouds and gray skies. I appreciate my job, but I am asking that my superiors, coworkers, and staff be considerate. Give us a positive work environment where we all compliment and praise each other. Lord, I pray we could just treat others how we want to be treated. In Jesus' name. Amen.

Ecclesiastes 2:22–25 (ESV)

What has a man from all the toil and striving of heart with which he toils beneath the sun? For all his days are full of sorrow, and his work is a vexation. Even in the night his heart does not rest. This also is vanity. There is nothing better for a person than that he should eat and drink and find enjoyment in his toil. This also, I saw, is from the hand of God, for apart from him who can eat or who can have enjoyment?

DAY 89

Today I am saying no to self-sabotage. I can do it, I will do it, and I deserve the best because I am the best. (I am God-approved!)

Today, I said no to:

_____

_____

_____

_____

_____

Why did I say no?

_____

_____

_____

_____

_____

Saying no made me feel:

- o Independent
- o Strong
- o Guilty
- o Mean
- o Happy
- o Empowered
- o _____

My no gave me more:

- Time
- Opportunity
- Satisfaction
- Power
- Anxiety

I am now available to say yes to or to do:

_____

_____

_____

_____

_____

Prayer

Lord, please remove all doubts about my own abilities from my mind. I know it is only fear that keeps me paralyzed. I fear being criticized by others. Lord, I have faith in You. Help me step out. You said I should not hide my light but let it shine. Remove the fear. Remove any excuses I can put before me to explain away the talents You have placed inside me. You made me to shine in Your light and I intend to do just that. With You in me, nothing is impossible. Win or lose, You get the glory, and I am still a winner in Your eyes. In Jesus' name. Amen.

- ✓ I am a light that shines brightly.
- ✓ I am super talented and gifted.
- ✓ I am not afraid of other seeing my God-given talent.

Matthew 5:15 (ESV)

Nor do people light a lamp and put it under a basket, but on a stand, and it gives light to all in the house.

DAY 90--I MADE IT!

Today and for the rest of my life, I am reclaiming my right to say yes and no! I am saying no to anything toxic in my life, which creates toxic feelings and toxic habits! I am enough. I am not too much. I am worthy. I am blessed. I am beautiful. From now on, I am saying no to mess and stress so I can say yes to my success!

My biggest things I said no to in 90-Days were:

1. _____
2. _____
3. _____
4. _____
5. _____
6. _____
7. _____
8. _____
9. _____
10. _____

Saying no made me feel:

- ○ Independent
- ○ Strong
- ○ Amazing
- ○ In Control
- ○ Happy
- ○ Empowered
- ○ _____

Saying no gave me more:

- ○ Time
- ○ Opportunity
- ○ Satisfaction
- ○ Power
- ○ Self-Love

Prayer

Lord, I made it through. I am a finisher. I am worthy. I am not a doormat for people to walk on. My feelings do matter, they are valid, and they do count. I should be able to say no without it being held against me by others or by myself. I should be able to say yes and feel good about my choice. Protect my heart. Give me all the love and support You know I need. Surround me with people who will protect me and respect and honor our friendship. People who love me and have my best interest at heart. Give me a job and a ministry that wants to help others by asking what they need and working with them to reach their goals. I love the giving heart that You have blessed me with. I want to use it to serve You. Help me protect it by protecting my no and preserving my yes for the appropriate time. In Jesus' name. Amen.

Joshua 1:9 (NIV)

Have I not commanded you? Be strong and courageous. Do not be afraid; do not be discouraged, for the Lord your God will be with you wherever you go.

You've reached the end of Day 90. Take a moment to write your own prayer or tell how God is leading you on your NO Journey:

_____

_____

_____

_____

_____

_____

_____

_____

_____

_____

_____

_____

_____

_____

_____

_____

_____

_____

_____

_____

_____

You Did It

No

Nope

Nada

Nuh uh

Nah

———————

The end.

Made in the USA
Monee, IL
01 June 2023

34905181R00125